Decision According to Law

By the same author:

Capital Punishment
The Inevitability of Caprice and Mistake

CHARLES L. BLACK Jr.

Decision According to Law

The 1979 Holmes Lectures

W · W · NORTON & COMPANY

NEW YORK · LONDON

Library of Congress Cataloging in Publication Data
Black, Charles Lund, 1915–
    Decision according to law.
    (The Holmes lectures; 1979)
    1. Judicial power—United States.   2. Judicial process—United
States.   3. United States. Supreme Court.   4. Judicial review—United
States.   I. Title.   II. Series: Oliver Wendell Holmes lectures;
1979.   KF5130.B55   347.73'12   80–39852   ISBN 0–393–01452–5

W. W. Norton & Company, Inc. 500 Fifth Avenue, New York, N.Y. 10110
W. W. Norton & Company Ltd. 25 New Street Square, London EC4A 3NT

1 2 3 4 5 6 7 8 9 0

To DAVID ALAN BLACK:

"Your quest is my well
 Of desired water, the gate
 Of my city unremoved."

Preface

My thanks go first to the Harvard Law School faculty and staff, for their honoring me with their invitation to be their Holmes Lecturer in 1979, and for the crowd of kindnesses in my entertainment there in April of that year. The occasion seemed in one way a sort of three-day party for the Black and Aronstein families, a feast not alone of reason, a flow of soul only if one takes that word in a spacious sense that reaches to friendship. I used to hear some people say that the Harvard Law School was a frowning, forbidding place. Those people must have been thinking about some other institution.

I came away especially grateful to Dean Albert Sacks, whose magically gracious touch was everywhere; to Professor Henry Steiner, who played an especially important part in making my stay a pleasant one; to Elisabeth Wahlen and Donna Chiozzi, who contrived that what must have been the most painstaking arrangements seemed as though they had been brought about by the wave of a wand.

Back home, I give my thanks to Dean Harry Wellington for his continual help and support, in this as in so many things; to Arthur Charpentier, the best of librarians; to Gene Coakley, who always gets the book there two minutes before you ask for it; most especially to Elizabeth Modena, for her skilful management of the manuscript, from first yellow-pad scrawl to last footnote in place.

My thanks go to George P. Brockway, for his constant encouragement and support; to Josepha Gutelius, for most helpful editorial work; and to Andrew J. Marasia, production manager—all of W. W. Norton & Company.

And of course to Barbara Aronstein Black (if I may be permitted to say so once again, with eleven years' more reason than when I first said it) for everything.

C. L. B., JR.

Decision According to Law

Introduction

What follows is the text of the Oliver Wendell Holmes Lectures, delivered, on two April evenings in 1979, at the Harvard Law School.

When I came square up against the necessity of fitting the prepared matter of those lectures into bearable length for delivery on two evenings, I found I had to cut out a great deal of introductory material. Some of it was merely interesting, at least to me. Some of it could have been, I judge, a help to understanding what followed. I hope the highly specialized audience at Harvard did not suffer too much; in any case that's past and done. But I have thought it wise to put, before this lecture-text in this book, some explanation of how it happens that one could think it urgent to explore the problem of "Decision According to Law"—how it is that this concept connects with the intense scholarly and public attention that is now attracted to the place and work of the courts—with the Supreme Court at the top of judgment.

There are four themes that must be connected with one another. It will conduce to clarity if I set each of these out briefly, before I try to develop each as needful, show their interworkings, and so lead up to the chief matter of the text.

First, there are the highly visible prominence and importance of the courts, as part of our political system. Here I shall be attending mainly to the work of the Supreme Court as the place of final judgment on all those questions of prudence and value which we see as "constitutional" questions. I shall not be looking north or south or across either sea, so you will have to take my word for it, for now, that this placing and empowerment of the judiciary is a specific difference that marks our American polity off from most others. Our commitment to judicial power has been, and remains, the wonder of the world.

Secondly, there is the problem of the consonance of this judicial powerfulness with democracy. Federal judges, including those on the Supreme Court, are not elected by the people, and are tenured for life. Although the average term of service has been surprisingly short, the crucial fact is that no federal judge ever faces or anticipates facing an election of any kind. There appears in this an absolutely prime problem as to the democratic character of our government, a problem that will not go away just because we are used to this position.

Thirdly, there is the problem of the power of the national Congress over the jurisdiction and procedures of the federal courts. If you think about the first and second themes, you can see that the manner of resolution of this third theme could have a lot to do with answering the question whether the tension between great power in judges, and total lack of electoral responsibility in judges, is tolerable in a democracy.

Fourthly, there is the problem—my central problem in what follows—of "decision according to law." Our courts present themselves as reaching decision "according to law." We call on our fellow-citizens for obedience to court judgments on the ground of their being decided, at least in good-faith attempt, "according to law." But the insights of the last hundred years have shown this concept to be not a simple, but a highly problematic one. What is it to decide "according to law"—as distinguished from other modes and grounds of decision?

Now let me develop each of these themes a little further.

As to the momentous weight of judicial power: We have lately learned some things either new or known before and forgotten. Some of these things are not frail footnotes to footnotes, but insights of strategic import. They master our 1981 perceptions of the place of judicially wrought constitutional law in our lives. The greatest difference between us seniors and our students is that to them, overall, these insights are a part of the given, while to us they are the products of change from what was the given thirty years ago.

We have learned, first and most important, that people were wrong who said that courts' actions could not have very much effect on life outside court. I could rest the case for this on the decision in *Brown v. Board of Education*,[1] the decision that brought down the Southern segregation system.

Some people say, or seem to say, that the *Brown* case had little effect. I have said "seem to say," because I have to wonder whether I literally so much as understand the position thus taken. Before *Brown*, there was, in a large section of the United States, a well-masoned Cyclopean wall of racial segregation by law, scribbled over with insult to millions of blacks, and shutting millions of whites away from the well of human kindness. *Brown* knocked down that wall. The Southern segregation system no longer exists *in specie*; bits and pieces of it, some quite big, still lie about, but the system is gone. In the case of a ship analogously damaged, the insurer on hull would pay as for a

---

1. 347 U.S. 483 (1954). In this case, the segregation of blacks in public education was declared unconstitutional. The holding in the case was speedily generalized to cover all forms of racial segregation imposed by law. Before this decision, the whole of life in the American South was dominated by the practice of racial segregation, from cradle to grave.

total loss, even though the Coast Guard might still be busy
removing the wreck. Within about fifteen years after *Brown*, the
principal characteristic of the social and legal structure of a vast
region had been wiped out. When the validation of supporting
law is swept away by a judicial decision, and when you observe a
few years later that the system, as a pervasive Southwide system,
is simply gone, not there anymore, is there not an irresistible
suggestion that the removal of the validation had a good deal to
do with the disappearance?

Curiously, I don't find that the people who assail the
Brown decision, as being without fruit, concentrate upon this
question of causality; they seem rather to be saying that nothing
much has happened since *Brown*, in the area which *Brown*
touched. This view could be held, I must respectfully say, only
by somebody who wasn't there in the old times. The change is
massive, one of the most massive social changes ever doc-
umented for so many people over a like period of time—one
of the greatest changes in history occurring in so short a time
and not resulting from war or preparation for war. The Southern segregation system was not the only thing demolished; the
cardinal tenet of the old Sumnerian legal sociology, the
sociological tenet both underlying and rising to expression in
that most sociological of opinions, *Plessy v. Ferguson*[2]—the
proposition that "law-ways cannot change folk-ways"—has
been stunned into a silence rather resembling death.

About five years ago, and so not much more than twenty
years after the *Brown* decision, I went down to Austin, Texas,
my old home, to testify on a death-penalty bill pending before a
state legislative committee. Between committee sessions I went
to eat in a middle-sized café near the Capitol. A black family,

---

2. 163 U.S. 537 (1896). This case was the legal cornerstone of the segregation
system. It upheld a Louisiana law requiring segregation in railroad cars, but it was
conventionally generalized to sanction all forms of segregation imposed by law.

parents and several children, came in, took a table, dealt with the children's disputes over seating, and started studying the menu. When I was young, a black family that tried this would have been lucky to escape without serious injury. I sat quietly, with that tingling feeling in the neck—the very feeling by which (I think it is Housman who says) we recognize poetry that works. It may not mean much to sit down in that café. It meant a lot not to be allowed to sit down there with your children—generation after generation.

I often ask people who write off the *Brown* case to give me an example of a *successful* case—of a judgment that did a whole lot more good than *Brown*. Having heard no satisfying reply, I rashly trust my own recollection enough to say that, far from being a failure, *Brown* did more good than any other judicial decision ever uttered.

The *Brown* case had vast tangible effects, particularly if you trace them, as certainly you must, into all parts of life. You can read them easily on the faces of people in a restaurant in Austin; the food and the ambient are a bit of an improvement upon the old times of three cracked stools in a dingy little room behind the kitchen in the Austin bus station. But to stop there would do the case much less than justice. The *Brown* case was already a success—and herein is a wonderful truth about law—on the day that the first school board told the first lie to balk desegregation of its schools. The telling of that lie marked a great change, the Great Divide. The day before *Brown*, the political society in which black people lived had determined, in its highest court, that insulting them, by public law, was lawful; the word "segregation" was written among the stars on the flag. From about noon, on May 17, 1954, the stars sang a different word—a word even now hard to make out, but certainly very different; the flag was in other hands. However fierce the battle was to be, the political society had held, in its highest court, that the old insult was no part of its law. The day before *Brown*, that school board was supported by all of us, through our legitimate organs of judgment. The day after *Brown*, nothing but lies would do.

A second stunning example of judicial effectiveness is the "reapportionment" line of cases—forcing approximate population equality in legislative districts.[3] The political map of the country was totally redrawn in ten years, quite plainly in consequence of judicial action. Out of these reapportionment cases, moreover, two other absolutely cardinal lessons were firmly learned.

It was discovered that, at least sometimes, courts could effect vast political change without provoking vast political opposition. Before *Baker v. Carr*,[4] to believe that entering the apportionment field would involve the judiciary in disastrous political conflict was a shibboleth of true faith for the right-minded. No warnings were ever given with more confidence; none was ever wronger. The process gave the sociologists—after the fact, of course—a new concept, "hidden consensus."

Out of the same cases, we learned another lesson, one we should not have had to learn so late: Judges do not dislike power, any more than other people do. There is a paradox here; we are given a look into the complexity of institutional forces. Some of the ablest and most dedicated of our judges—of course I have in mind Mr. Justice Frankfurter, but a number of others could be included—had so faithfully illustrated the virtue of judicial forbearance that they convinced a good many of us, much contrary to their own intent or desire, that there was little risk in

3. The leading case on this was *Baker v. Carr*, 369 U.S. 186 (1962). The actual holding in this opinion was only that the courts had power to hear and determine suits complaining of inequality in populations of legislative districts. The decision was soon implemented and generalized in a large number of Supreme Court holdings.

4. See note 3 above.

putting great power within the reach of the judiciary; the *nolo episcopari*, we feared and believed, would be only too heartfelt. Early comment on *Baker v. Carr* illustrates this; all or almost all of this, my own included, either asserted or, more significantly, assumed that the implementation of *Baker* would be mild, both as to the stringency of standards and as to the drasticness and pacing of relief. Hardly ever has a prediction, or an assumption about the future, been more mistaken. On the whole, the federal judiciary took up the redistricting job with sharpest relish, applied the strictest standards with an air of correcting the most blameworthy of wanton wrongdoers, and moved with utterly unforeseen speed to the drastic remedies of elections-at-large and redistricting by judicial decree, rather in the manner of one who has enjoyed a hearty breakfast and wants to work up an appetite for lunch. They loved it.

These three lessons, firmly learned in the decades just past, make a cluster: Judicial power can be effective, even in the largest matters; warnings of unacceptable political turmoil, in consequence of judicial activity, are quite unreliable; and many judges greatly like power, and eagerly use it.

These three perceptions have put all questions about the judicial function into an altogether new frame. They make a cluster because, together, they warn us that we are dealing here with forces of great strength, far greater than we knew before.

As for the second theme—the problem of the inconsonance with democracy of the exercise of great power over public matters by life-tenured judges—I think no elaboration is necessary. The clearest course will be for me to bridge over to the third theme and state the thesis I have defended elsewhere and shall defend in the main text that follows: There is no way to resolve this inconsonance unless the body that represents the national democracy—Congress—has considerable power over the jurisdiction of the courts. I would only add that the first theme, above, makes it clear how important this problem is. Our life-tenured judges are not in the business of deciding only such issues as "Who has title to this automobile?" They are dealing from a position of final authority over such questions as the racial composition of the public schools, the permissible means of defense against street crime, the relations between church and state, the make-up of congressional districts, the practical scope of the right to choose abortion, the powers of the president in national crisis. In managing such high matters— and this makes the conflict between judicial power and democracy an agonizing one—they are often not merely bypassing the democratically elected legislatures, but are even annulling and undoing the provisions set in force by these legislatures.

The third problem, then—the problem of the power of Congress over the jurisdiction of the federal courts, including the Supreme Court—I see as absolutely vital. "Jurisdiction" is the *power to decide*. If Congress has wide and deep-going power over the courts' *jurisdiction*, then the courts' *power to decide* is a continuing and visible concession from a democratically formed Congress. If Congress's power is severely limited, so that the judges' power to decide is theirs by indefeasible constitutional right, beyond the reach of Congress, then the vast judicial power we now see exercised was given once and for all when the Constitution came into effect, almost two hundred years ago, and is in no categorically statable way supported by any action since then, on the part of the organs of democracy. This is not, to me, an acceptable position. I would despair of defending the judicial power, as we now see and know it, if I believed that the national Congress had no choice but to let the courts perpetually enjoy such power as the courts themselves might hold to be theirs. My own position is—and I defend it in what follows—that Congress does have very significant power over the courts' jurisdiction.

Perhaps it would be well to put before you at once the textual constitutional material that this problem implicates. Article III of the Constitution empowers Congress to "ordain and establish" such lower courts as it may "from time to time" see fit to establish, and gives the Supreme Court "appellate jurisdiction, with such exceptions and under such regulations as Congress may make."[5] I believe it is fair to say that, until the last few decades, the great weight of authority and competent opinion has been to the effect that the power to "ordain and establish" the lower courts includes the power to bestow upon them such and only such jurisdiction as Congress desires, "from time to time," and that the power to make "exceptions" to the appellate jurisdiction of the Supreme Court is a power to make such exceptions to that jurisdiction as Congress thinks it wise to make. Doubts as to the deep and broad reach of these congressional powers are on the whole of fairly recent origin.

It may be clarifying, too, if I point out the difference between a congressional power over *jurisdiction* and a congressional power to tell the courts *how to decide constitutional questions*, when these come before the courts in the exercise of the jurisdiction they are given. I would say, and always have said, that Congress might validly (though of course in my view most wrongly) have abolished the *jurisdiction* of the federal courts over school segregation cases—but Congress could not first direct the courts to take jurisdiction over such cases, and then direct the courts to decide that segregation did not violate the Constitution. As with all distinctions, close cases can be imagined as to this distinction, but the main areas are clear.

This brings us up to the fourth problem—central to the task addressed in the following text—of "decision according to law." What does the prepositional phrase, *"according to,"* mean in this formula?

5. See U.S. CONSTITUTION, Article III.

There is no telling whether any really informed and intelligent observer ever quite fully believed that the courts did or can or ought to decide all cases and all questions as an act of obedience to clearly ascertainable commands of law, without there entering anything like the judges' "will."[6] The important thing now is that the most fundamental work of our century on the nature and functioning of law has demonstrated, to the satisfaction of virtually every competent student, that this picture is illusory. The point is not that, although definite "law," susceptible of being definitely obeyed, is *there*, it is very hard to discover, so that judges make many mistakes; it is rather that the very nature of the material we call "law," of the material we look to when we look for "law," and of the methods we use in this search for right "law," are such that they very often make it not merely *possible* but *inevitable* that the beliefs and even the feelings of the judge go into the making of judgment. This is true because the whole body of "law," separate from those beliefs and feelings—even if fully known and handled with the highest expertness—very often does not suffice to lead the mind, by scientific or logical manipulations, to an unequivocally established right result, and must in the nature of things fail to do this.

I shall be dealing with the problem of harmonizing the institution of judicial review, in reference to the assumptions and rationalia that underlie its legitimation, with these insights of the past century into the intellectual placing of law.

There are some things that "decision according to law" cannot be. Everything we know of law, through all time and among all peoples, warns us that we must not look, in its

6. In THE FEDERALIST PAPERS, Number 78, Alexander Hamilton said that the judiciary had "neither FORCE nor WILL, but merely judgment. . . ." But the word "judgment" itself is not self-explanatory, nor does it self-evidently exclude "will" in every possible sense.

reasonings, for the rigor of mathematics or of the sciences. I am not sure whether Aristotle, in saying this about political argument, would have included legal argument in this political category, but he should have. I am not even sure that he would have seen a difference; in ancient Athens, a political question often became a judicial question and, as in other places, a judicial question often became a political question.

The insight ought not to be taken as a plea for toleration of insufficient reason. If it were that only, it might well be omitted as deplorably unnecessary, today or in any other day. It is not at all an apology for insufficient reason, but an insistence that the *nature of sufficiency* in legal reasonings be recognized, so that such sufficiency may be more well-directly sought and thus more often attained. If "decision according to law" can mean no more than choice among arguments and considerations, none of which is geometrically decisive, on the basis of their persuasiveness as best we can assess it, then, by a natural and healthful reversal, our concern must be that decision according to law be no *less* than this—a very heavy demand, for it must lead to more rather than to less thoroughness in the consideration that goes into judgment, to more rather than to less fullness and clarity in reasons given. Quantitative analysis is harder and closer work than qualitative analysis.

Imagining a tunnel does not ensure emergence into light. But the possibility does suggest itself here that the seeming trend away from rationality in our century may have been an indispensable ground-clearing for the construction of a new rationality, based not on the concept of cogency but on the concept of competing assessment. If the life of the law cannot be logic in the traditional sense, but must be experience, or a sense of expediency, or these two and some other things beyond the older logic, then what we need is a new logic, not merely imaginable but reflex-habitual, wherein may naturally be accommodated the realities of assessing persuasive power on a scale more finely graded than the primitive logical scale of T and F.

As I say this, I am reminded of Holmes's words, "We too need education in the obvious." The syllogism still rules us from its grave. Those of us who desire a new life for the concept of decision according to law must constantly remind ourselves that the older and simpler concepts are no longer living.

The most rigorous approach to this problem goes through the study of language. "Argument," says the Taoist sage, "is the relation in time of one mutable sound to another."[7] Language is the linseed oil of law. We have to use linseed oil in painting; when exposed to air it hardens to a nearly transparent substance that holds in place for centuries the very molecules of pigment that were in the mess smeared on. But it yellows, it cracks, and it peels—rather badly, sometimes, however careful you are, and quite badly, much of the time, if you are not careful. In one way or another law not only *uses* language, but may be said only to exist in language; the dangers of language are dangers to law.

And there is a special point about legal language, a point that grows in importance as that language becomes more and more general, as in such phrases as "due process of law" and "privileges and immunities of citizens." In 1923 C. K. Ogden and I. A. Richards published what was to become a seminal book to the world—*The Meaning of Meaning*. A "triangle" in that book, possibly the third most famous triangle in history (I am thinking of course of the Eternal Triangle and of the Pythagorean right triangle) put the user or hearer of a verbal symbol at the top angle, the verbal symbol at one of the base angles, and the thing or event referred to at the other base angle.

7. Chuang Chou, in CHINESE PHILOSOPHY IN CLASSICAL TIMES (E. R. Hughes ed. and trans.) (Everyman Series, 1942), p. 183.

The base of the triangle was not filled in; thus the authors made graphic the insight that there is no independent connection between the word—the "sounds mutable in time"—and the thing or event referred to. The connection exists only in and through the nervous systems of the users and hearers of the language. Words have no inherent, natural, proper meaning.

The trouble is that most of the people in whose "intent" we are interested, as being by convention determinant of the fictive intent of some collectivity, such as "Congress," did not read that book. A part of their mental state on using a word or a phrase—the mental state that is at the apex of the baseless triangle—may therefore have been a belief—the very belief that Ogden and Richards thought widespread enough to require their striving to dispel it—that there *was* a base to the triangle—that expressions like "privileges and immunities of citizens of the United States" *did* have a natural and proper meaning, to be worked out as we go along. Or perhaps some of them thought, as I think and as most courts even now seem to think, that the best results would often be attained if we behaved *as if* the bottom of the triangle were filled in.

If, then, constitutional law entailed no more than the choice of "meanings" in the text, it would have large leeways, wherein the text could not be heard to speak with clarity. But constitutional law, like all law, employs methods beyond textual interpretation—the method of *analogy* with the textual provision, the method of inference from the structures and relationships created by the text, and—in developed law—the method of following precedent. All these methods are copiously used in constitutional law, as in other law, in patterns of coaction that vary widely. But discordant opinions are possible, in good faith and with no suggestion of technical imcompetence on anybody's part, as to the persuasiveness of an urged analogy, or of a pressed suggestion of inference from structure

and relationship, or of a precedent. Choice among these discordant opinions can be made, I think, in three ways: by some
mode of casting lots; by self-deluding unconscious impulse; or
by disciplined and insightful choice amongst the competing
values and expediences, marshaled and structured as best they
may be.

I would make the point very strongly that this situation is in
no way peculiar to American constitutional law. As far as we
can tell, all law, among all peoples, always has been and always
will be like this. There is no ground for hope that we can have a
constitutional law without these characteristics. If we are going
to commit questions of constitutional law to the courts, then we
are going to commit such questions to a process of judicial
decision that has these leeways, and so calls for judgments of
rightness, fitness, justice, on the part of the judges.

On the other hand, these insights about law have a special
relevance to the functioning of the courts in all constitutional
cases that involve scrutiny and possible overturning of a legislative judgment already rendered. We now know that, in such a
case, the court is substituting its own judgment, as to what
ought to fill in the leeways of constitutional law, for that which
has been (or at least may have been) made by the legislative
body. (I have inserted the reservation, "may have been," because very often there is no positive evidence that the affected
legislative body has raised and faced the judgment of rightness,
as being one to be made in the interstices of constitutional law.)

It should be made explicit, as well, that this problem has
many modes and shadings. At one end, there may be a problem
of "interpretation" of a term not very complex or vague. For
example, is a corporate charter a "contract" between the incorporators and the state that grants the charter, within the meaning of the constitutional provision forbidding impairment of

"the obligation of a contract"?[8] Or, even more narrowly, have the emoluments of an office "been increased *during*" a senator's term in the Senate if the salary of the office was raised in the course of that term, but lowered to its original level before the term ended?[9]

On the other hand, the question may be, "What are the privileges and immunities belonging to a citizen of the United States"?[10] Or "What are the 'other rights' mentioned in the Ninth Amendment,[11] and are they to be given force as law by the courts?" Cases and questions fall all along the line established here.

It is important to note this, because it is only with the more spacious questions, resting on vague provisions, that any distinction at all (and that a very dubious one) can be drawn between the tone and texture of constitutional law and those of other law. Ordinary law courts decide, every day in their routine, questions of the "contract" kind or the "increased emoluments" kind. This spectrum, this gradient of generality and its associated vagueness, will be of importance in what follows. It cannot hurt to say, even here, that, while a good deal of the skeptical literature on judicial review has seized on the courts' discerning of protectible interests in the most general of language, a surprisingly small part of the politically controversial judicial work has actually been of this kind; most of that work has consisted in the filling out, the making specific, of rights (fair procedure in criminal trials, immunity from coercion as to religion, immunity from racial discrimination, the

8. See U.S. CONSTITUTION, Article I, Section 10, and *Dartmouth College v. Woodward*, 4 Wheaton 518 (U.S. Supreme Court, 1819).

9. See U.S. CONSTITUTION, Article I, Section 6.

10. U.S. CONSTITUTION, Amendment XIV, Section 1.

11. U.S. CONSTITUTION, Amendment IX. See *infra* at p. 43 and following.

right to free expression) that have the firmest constitutional warrant, quite apart from the most general matter in the constitutional text, and need only be worked into concreteness by the courts.

Now let me pick up all these four themes, and put them into the form of a set of ideas which the text that follows will seek to support.

Our courts of law, headed by the Supreme Court, exert an enormous power over the practical and moral shape of the nation. This power is exerted by appointed tenured judges, related to the electorate only indirectly in their appointment, and not at all so related once they take office. This power has as its principal ingredient the power to overturn and nullify judgments of people who are regularly elected, and commonly want to be reelected. This power is exerted in the name of *law*, but we now know (whether or not people knew in 1787) that the judge who decides the cases under law *cannot avoid* making— and acting upon—judgments of justice, morality, expediency, fitness.

That tenured judges should enjoy such power, on the basis of "law" so understood, is to me a thing not to be accepted just because it was brought into being in 1788. Nor could I be satisfied with a fictitious or mystical "popular consent," not expressed in a positive way by the people's elected representatives. I think the whole apparatus should be dismantled unless one can say (as I do say) that Congress, representing the democracy from year to year, right now in 1981 could seriously diminish this allocation of policy power to tenured judges, and has instead chosen, and still chooses, not to do so.

If judicial review is thus in the hand of the democracy, then I think the question changes altogether. It is not necessarily unreasonable for a democracy to decide to keep on, from year to year, entrusting tenured people with jurisdiction to decide the questions our Supreme Court decides. Indeed, if Congress could do otherwise, and *chooses* to make this commitment, then those who would fault this decision themselves have a problem with the postulates of democracy. They are assailing as undemocratic a decision the democracy has made and can reverse at any time.

Nevertheless, one question remains: Is this congressional entrustment of power to the Court the result of sham, of an induced illusion that there is serious meaning in the idea of "decision according to law"? It is this question, principally, that I explored in the Holmes Lectures in the text that follows.

The question remains a solemn one, even if we see the institution of judicial review as being continually and freshly legitimated by democratic consent, because we must always be vigilant to be sure that this consent is not the result of a huge (and even an induced) mistake, on the part of the people and their representatives, as to the nature of the judicial work in constitutional cases.

The public obligations of students of constitutional law seem to me to be rather complex. No two students may see this matter exactly alike, but these are the ways I see it:

First, there is the obligation of *assessing*—and of continually reassessing—the position, in respect of the component or factor of *lawfulness* in this work of the judiciary, as it is performed.

Secondly, there is the obligation of *communicating* to one's fellow-citizens, as best one can, the thoughts and evaluations resulting (from time to time) in this continual process of assessment.

Thirdly, there is the obligation of *contributing*, when one can, to the maximization of this quality of lawfulness in the courts' work.

All these obligations—and the complex they form—are

vague of outline. That is not really a decisive objection to our trying to fulfill them. They are not as vague or elusive as the obligation of assessing, say, the *justice* of decisions, or of communicating to one's fellows the results of this assessment, or of seeking to contribute what thoughts one has toward the goal of greater justice. The idea of "decision according to law," like the idea of "justice," is too great an idea to give up just because we cannot pin it down with absolute clarity.

These three obligations are to be discharged by seeking, explaining, and guarding the component of lawfulness in constitutional decision. The text that follows is an enterprise of this kind. I hope it may be helpful to some who desire to go on thinking about the validity of the concept of "decision according to law." For all I can now see, that *desire*, leading to continual critical thought, is all we can have for the present. Maybe the thought of some future age will establish very clearly that this whole enterprise is hopeless—that "decision according to law" is a mere imagination. Or possibly some future age will see that we already had this great good, just because we wanted it and worked for it—that "decision according to law" is decision arrived at by such work, guided by such desire.

But for us now there is nothing to do but get on with it—unless we are ready to give up the idea altogether. I am not ready to do that. I think we have—in this matter as in others of comparable seriousness—not enough to be satisfied with, but enough to go on with.

Decision According to Law

It happened that I began to sketch these lectures on the very same September day of equinox when I passed out of that fearfully and wonderfully named Year of the Grand Climacteric, into the first hours of autumn. This circumstance seemed to me so full of fate that I was inspired to compose a proemium of some six or seven pages, filled with long reflections on the uses of astrology and the Book of Changes. I am sorry to have had to cancel all that. Some other time, perhaps. I also had to excise an exploration of our own generation's changes in the perception of judicial power. We veterans owe it to the fresher troops to try to convey to them the feeling of the times before the *Brown* case,[12] when it was thought in the schools that judicial activity could not really do much good; the times before *Baker v. Carr*,[13] when it was thought that any deep judicial interference in political matters would surely provoke uncontrollable violent reaction; the times, before a great many cases, when it

12. *Brown v. Board of Education*, 347 U.S. 483 (1954)—the great leading case outlawing segregation of blacks. For fuller treatment, see the Introduction, *supra*, p. 13.

13. 369 U.S. 186 (1962)—holding that inequalities in legislative district populations could be inquired into and remedied by the courts. This case was followed by many others, imposing stringent requirements of equal-population districts, for state legislatures and for the national House of Representatives. See Introduction, *supra*, p. 16.

was thought that judges, unlike other people, didn't care much for power. [14] All this had to be struck out, whether lamentably or not one will never know.

Yet another thirty pages tried to give shape to that intellectual and high-political field of forces which judicial decision now forms; herein was much said of the "normative power of the actual," considered not as a thing always disfavoring change, but as an inertial principle of at least Newtonian generality, inhibiting change but also keeping change in motion once it has begun—with copious illustrations.

All that too had to go. With it went—and here I confess a breach of warranty, I hope not material—the two-part and two-title plan with which I started, and in which I persevered, though with forebodings of abridgment to come, until after the invitations and posters had congealed into print. [15] When I got down to the stern court of minutes and words, I found there was to be no room for introductory material. The only way I could have saved it all—astrology and the I Ching, the radical transformation in what the Court seemed to be, the general theory of the "normative power of the actual," and a good deal of other matter of that sort—was to give three lectures, and as to that I took to heart in season the counsel of others, and remembered as well Saint Paul, who listed faith, hope, and charity, but had the judgment to discourse *in extenso* on only two of these. So what I have for you is a pair of lectures pretty much on the second of the topics I announced before the metal had hardened.

In that commonest of time's heartbreaking paradoxes, both few and many years have passed since I wrote these words:

14. See Introduction, *supra*, pp. 16–17.

15. The eventual title, *Decision According to Law*, was to have been the title of the last of two lectures—before the realism of time took final effect. The "lectures" thus became, really, one lecture, with a mere reel-change about midway, between the first and second evenings.

The concept of "decision according to law" is one of the most consecrated inheritances of our culture. Without it, we would be something very different from what we are; perhaps our culture could not live at all. We will give it up only if it is demonstrated beyond hope to be untenable. The last fifty years have shown it not to be tenable in the naive form in which most people conceived it in the nineteenth century; law is not a matter of sure professional reasoning to demonstratedly valid conclusions, on the base of cases and texts of authority, without any reference to the judge's sense of right. In 1961 we have to ask ourselves: "If not that, then what? What is it to decide according to law? What livable shape can be given to this concept?"

The best thing any fifty years can give to the next fifty is a problem like that.[16]

The problem I touched on then has been put by others in other words.[17] I still think it best to speak of "decision according to law." That phrase can only name an aspiration not sure of the direction or locus of its goal. This makes it all the more fitting for the place in which we do presently stand. Its highest value lies in its referring not to an extrinsic concept or system but to the art of law itself; law, though drawing help from everywhere, is to be validated by its own laws.

We all have dreams of glory. None is fairer than the one we dream just before the Number Two pencil rides off on its quest through the yellow pad, in pursuit of a solution to such a problem as the one enfolded in the passage I have read you. But we come awake. I cannot lead myself, and so cannot lead you, to a clean-lined post-skeptical[18] conception of decision according to law. I only long for lawfulness in law's work. I am sure

16. From *Changing and Unchanging Faces of Law*, YALE REV., Autumn 1961, reprinted in BLACK, THE OCCASIONS OF JUSTICE, pp. 3, 15 (1963).

17. See WECHSLER, "Toward Neutral Principles of Constitutional Law," in his PRINCIPLES, POULITICS AND FUNDAMENTAL LAW, pp. 4–10; also ELY, DEMOCRACY AND DISTRUST, especially pp. 11–72 (1980).

18. See Introduction, *supra*, at pp. 19 ff.

many of you long for it as well. This longing, and the longing for justice, are the noblest emotions of law. From their tension, their seeming contradiction, the art of law takes its life, as the art of archery takes its life from the opposition of the string and the bow, neither of which—and in this similitude I confess to my deepest faith concerning the ultimate grounds of our work—is any good without the other.

I have ended up with a modest plan. I shall take some problems in constitutional law, and try to show that they are susceptible of solution by methods that may at least point toward the quality of lawfulness. These few thrustings at this great problem can have at the most a suggestive outcome; I am not ready, nobody is ready, for a general theory of lawfulness in decision. Still, we may catch glimpses, if not of the goal, at least of the start of the road. The prospect is not full of glory. But it may not be a dream.

We have all accepted—if for no better reason than because we had to—the proposition that legal reasoning never can have the rigor of mathematics or of the firmer sciences; that proposition needs no advocacy in this day. I think one needful suggestion, just now, is that this view of the limits on legal reason, right though it surely be, carries dangers. Its acceptance may engender a disdain for the kind of reasoning (not always unattainable) that approaches fairly closely to the demonstrative. Sometimes the best way to judge the persuasive force of any line of reasoning is to develop it as though the goal of demonstrativeness, which can only be approached as a limit, and often not at all closely, were indeed touchable—though always, of course, with the knowledge that it is not. Any holding back in this regard pulls the wrong way; it frustrates assessment of the competing powers of contrary lines of thought, fully extended. At its worst it can make all arguments look pretty much alike.

I think these points have indirect relevance to some of the

comment on the *Brown* case,[19] the decision that opened our era of judicial activity. The *Brown* case is about as close to open-and-shut as a non-trivial decision at law can be. For full support, it needs only the two affirmances that the Fourteenth Amendment is to be taken as generally condemning the infliction of harm, by law, on blacks as blacks, and that segregation by law, in the notorious circumstances prevailing, was a harm.[20] These premises are a long way within the safe range of supportability in law. Yet I still encounter a puzzling reluctance to put them forward strongly, go with them all the way, and trust them. The *Brown* case is weakened, not strengthened, by the suggestion that its principal ground, as a decision at law, was an unprovable national moral consensus, in and around 1954.[21] For my part, I never in those days thought there was such a consensus. But, whatever I thought, the consensus was neither provable nor—more important—needed.[22]

But in what sense and in what degree is the *Brown* case exceptional? All questions in constitutional law cannot be as certain of answer as the question about Southern segregation. Can we hope to find a system of constitutional judgment that at least to a tolerable extent takes its decisions "according to law"?

Let me put a partial gloss on the word "tolerable." I think it possible that, after all that has been said,[23] the ideal of pre-formed law, wholly determinative of decision, still rules us from its grave, in that we feel a certain vague wrongness or lack about

19. The School Segregation Case of 1954. See Introduction, *supra* at pp. 13 ff; also *supra* at notes 1 and 12.

20. See Black, *The Lawfulness of the Segregation Decisions*, 69 YALE L. J. 421 (1960), reprinted in THE OCCASIONS OF JUSTICE (1963) at p. 129.

21. See BICKEL, THE LEAST DANGEROUS BRANCH 237–238 (1962) and John Ely's comment, *op. cit. supra* note 17, pp. 65–66.

22. Needed, that is to say, for establishing the rightness of the decision as a matter of law. Consensus was badly needed, and was at last formed, for the following out of the decision.

23. See Introduction, *supra* at p. 20.

our case-by-case failure to attain to this state of things—even though we know that it is not attainable and that its attainment is not desirable. Let us throw off this spectral rule. We can now perceive that the pursuit of lawfulness, of decision according to law, can mean only an attempt to build a system in which the element of reasoning from commitment *plays a part important enough* to mark a serious specific difference between decision according to law and other kinds of decision. No one now can sketch out generally the manner of entry of this component of lawfulness, its kind or degree, or its relations to other factors in the forming of judgment. The legitimate possibilities are various—after the manner more of variety in art than of variety in a game of well-constructed rules. But if we define the task in this way, we have not started by defining ourselves into despair.

This evening, I shall narrow the general question by placing it in a single context that brings it alive for me: Are the materials and methods available for the work of judicial review of such a nature as to make that function, in truth, no more than a disguised performance of legislative or administrative functions? Or is there—can there be—enough more to allow us honestly to present this work as different enough from other decisional work to justify the special authority-position it holds, and the validating ritual that surrounds it? (The very question makes me nervous enough to have to say—unsurprisingly, I am sure, to you—that there will be no answer in the back of this book.)

The most important breakdown of this question is the one that distinguishes among the authorities—state legislatures, Congress, or others—whose determinations are reviewed. Among the wondrous things about our discourse on judicial review, as it goes on through the long lapse of ages, is that, chronically, *semper et ubique et paene ab omnibus*, so little is made of the distinction, crucial practically to Holmes[24] and crucial theoretically to Thayer,[25] between review of *state* acts and review of *federal* acts. Time after time, in book after article, right down to the present, this unconditionally basic distinction is genuflected to hastily, as part of a prelude to a discussion that then blurs it as to all general issues.

The difference remains. Let me start with review of *state* acts. What can we say, first, about the legitimation of judicial review of acts taken under state authority?

The Constitution itself peremptorily commands that the Constitution prevail, in court, over state laws.[26] For some odd reason, there seems to subsist a fixed convention that the Article VI phrase, "Judges *in* the several States," shall not be interpreted (literally, sensibly, and in accordance with invariant assumption and practice, early and late) to include federal judges sitting "*in* the several States"—even though the 1787 Committee of Detail changed the language here from "the Judicatures *of* the several States" to the Article VI phrase.[27] But if the same result as the one reachable, even now, by a benign though belated literalness had not bounced back off the absurd-

24. "I do not think the United States would come to an end if we lost our power to declare an Act of Congress void. I do think the Union would be imperilled if we could not make that declaration as to the laws of the several States." HOLMES, COLLECTED LEGAL PAPERS 295 (1920).

25. Thayer, *The Origin and Scope of the American Doctrine of Constitutional Law*, 7 HARVARD L. REV. 129 at p. 154 (1893). Here Thayer, having said that an Act of Congress should be declared unconstitutional only if it is unconstitutional beyond any doubt, gives his reasons for judging that this rule should *not* apply to the claim that a state law offends the national Constitution.

26. "This Constitution, and the Laws of the United States which shall be made in Pursuance thereof; and all Treaties made, or which shall be made, under the Authority of the United States, shall be the supreme Law of the Land; and the Judges in every State shall be bound thereby, any Thing in the Constitution or Laws of any State to the Contrary notwithstanding."—U.S. CONSTITUTION, Article VI.

27. FARRAND, RECORDS OF THE FEDERAL CONVENTION, vol. ii, pp. 132 and 183.

ity of placing *federal* judges under a *lesser* obligation in this regard than those of the states, there would, even so, have been no reason for exempting the federal judges from obedience to the quite general mandate, addressed to all, that the Constitution shall be part of the "supreme Law of the Land."[28]

Straight away, in 1789, Congress directed the Supreme Court to supervise the state courts' compliance with Article VI.[29] In statutes passed shortly after the Civil War, in all instances more than one hundred years ago, Congress directed the lower federal courts, in very broad categories of cases, to supplement the state courts in this regard. These statutes have been kept up to date.[30]

Federal-on-state review, then, is legitimated much as the income tax is legitimated. It has a distinctly clearer base of legitimacy than the federal courts' function of finding and applying maritime law in general average cases. It has this clarity of claim not because of the academic community's ongoing assent to the rightness of asserted political or institutional estimates, but because the Constitution and laws say so. *Marbury v. Madison*[31] is stimulating to talk about, but its reasonings have nothing to do with the legitimacy of the great bulk of constitutional review—the kind of review that is by very far the most important kind.

Let me go on to another point about the authority-position

28. See the language quoted *supra*, note 26.
29. In the first national Judiciary Act, Section 25, Vol. 1 U.S. STATUTES AT LARGE, p. 85. This Section provided for review by the Supreme Court of any state case in which a state statute or other state action was upheld as against a claim of its invalidity by reason of repugnance to the national Constitution, laws or treaties.
30. See, e.g., 28 U.S. Code § 1343 (lower federal courts) and 28 U.S. Code § 1257 (Supreme Court review of state courts' determination of federal constitutional questions).
31. 1 Cranch 137 (1803). This case held (quite unsurprisingly at the time) that the courts, faced with an *Act of Congress* believed to violate the Constitution, must follow the Constitution, and treat the Act as void.

of the reviewing federal court when it is dealing with an action of the legislature of a state. It is crucially misleading, and in the simple sense simply wrong, to say of this relation that it differs from other judicial-legislative relations in that "the legislature" can, in all other cases than the constitutional case, revise and reverse the judicial judgment. On the contrary, as far as concerns any countering action by the *affected* legislature—the state legislature—the judicial action is of just the same finality in all cases applying federal law, from the "equal protection" clause,[32] through Acts of Congress and treaties, on down to the latest grazing regulation of the Department of the Interior. All a state legislature can do about a holding based on a federal statute is to try to get the law changed, in principle much as a large corporation or a trade association may try to get federal law changed. In the fully constitutional case—the decision in no way resting on anything Congress has done or not done—this petitioning or lobbying for repeal or other change is not of avail, as to the constitutional merits. This is a difference, but it is a difference as to the possibility of procuring corrective action from another legislative body, rather than a difference as to the possibility of corrective action by the affected legislature itself. There is nothing like a reversal of the natural order of authority between the judicial and the legislative branches.

This observation should lead us to notice a particular aspect of the question of the power of Congress over the federal courts' jurisdiction. If Congress does not have wide power over this jurisdiction, but is limited, as many now say, by an implicit constitutional reservation—roughly to the effect that all constitutional claims against the states must have a federal judicial forum for their assertion—the contradiction to democratic as-

32. In the Fourteenth Amendment. This clause is the fountainhead of racial equality under the Constitution.

sumptions is maximized. Consider the case in which a domi-
nant majority of the state legislatures, charged with the general
responsibility for order and justice, think that federal judicial
intervention in a certain field is of proven catastrophic consequence. Being obviously not empowered themselves to take
any action, they memorialize Congress. Congress, by large
majorities, and the president, agree with their judgment. If
some modern ideas are right, then even in such a case there
would be no power on earth that could do anything but continue to submit to the federal judicial jurisdiction as the judges
defined it—except by constitutional amendment, which can be
thwarted by thirty-four senators out of a hundred,[33] or by states
containing as few as nine million people.[34] I confess I am
staggered by the implied assertion, or assumption, that such a
position can be consonant with the root-ideas and greater say-
ings of democracy.

If, on the other hand, Congress has just about the power
that it seems to be given in the Constitution,[35] with no broad
implied limits on that power, then it is possible to say, to those
states passionately objecting to the activity of the federal courts
in respect of, let us say, the racial composition of school populations: "You are wrong in imagining an arrogation of power by
the courts. Look, it says in the United States Code[36] that the
federal courts are to take these cases and decide them according
to law as those courts see the law. If you think we are mis-

33. A constitutional amendment proposed by Congress must pass each House by a
two-thirds vote. U.S. CONSTITUTION, Article V.
34. This figure is the outcome of arithmetic on the 1970 census. Maybe by now it
would be ten million or even (though I doubt it) fifteen million.
35. In the passages quoted and discussed in the Introduction *supra* at pp. 18–19.
As brought out there, these passages seem on their face to give Congress very wide power
over the jurisdiction of the federal courts—the power, that is, to prescribe what *sorts of
cases those courts may hear*—not how they are to decide these cases.
36. See note 30 above.

construing the Code, try to get Congress to pass a clarifying amendment. If you think this congressional empowerment of the federal judiciary to be very unwise, then go to Congress and try to get them to change it. If Congress won't do either of these things, stop talking about usurpation, bootstraps, and especially about contradiction to democracy, because the national democracy, through its only voice, will have decided against you."

What we believe on this question of congressional power over jurisdiction makes a difference, above all, in the kind of law and legal method that is *tolerable,* as a basis for striking down actions of the states. In the farther ranges of legal indeterminacy, the range of as yet unestablished constitutional values, you are in one situation when you can say that Congress—not merely guessing, in the late eighteenth century, on the basis of eighteenth-century legal philosophy, what the work would be like,[37] but from time to time fully able to observe it, fully able to take into account all modern thought on the intellectual processes of legal decision[38]—*keeps in force* the direction that this work be done by the courts. You are in quite another situation when you have to say that the concept in the phrase "keeps in force" rests on a misapprehension which honesty requires be corrected, because Congress has no choice—and consequently the democracy has no choice. *For how many centuries do you think the existence of this uncheckable and self-defining judicial power would be consonant with democratic ideas?*

There is another problem as to this state material—one whose existence would alone suffice to make it absolutely essen-

37. See the quotation from THE FEDERALIST, *supra,* note 6.
38. See, Introduction, *supra* at p. 27; and see *infra* at note 158, for the general and very important application of this thought.

tial to observe the Holmes-Thayer distinction.[39] There may often be a paradox when the United States Supreme Court annuls an Act of Congress on some ground involving reliance at any juncture or in any way on a judgment regarding national ethical consensus. I shall later give at least one quite clear example to the contrary,[40] but generally there is a good deal in this point. But there is no suggestion at all of paradox in the mere fact that a state statute is annulled by the Court on grounds in some way implicating national consensus. Why should there be?

I do not mean to say that the concurrence of a large number of state legislatures in taking the same measure (if—as need not at all be the case—they sit in states containing a large majority of the people) can never be relevant on issues of national consensus. But even this matter has to be approached very carefully. I have some experience on this because of my long concern with the problem of state-legislature applications for a constitutional convention.[41] The entire strength and appeal of this movement rests on the perception that you can whoop and holler through a good many of the state legislatures' proposals that not only cannot be thought to have any chance in the national House—*wherein, alone among institutions, the American people are represented in proportion to their numbers*—but that couldn't even get anywhere in the Senate, where the states are equally represented. We have one of those going right now; if I look a little fatigued, that is why. The

39. The distinction, that is, between review of *state* acts for their consonance with the national Constitution, and the review of *national* acts, such as Acts of Congress, for this consonance. See *supra*, notes 24 and 25.

40. See *infra* at pp. 74–75.

41. Most recently in connection with the proposal of a "budget-balancing" amendment. See, generally, Black, *Amendment By National Constitutional Convention: A Letter to a Senator*, 32 OKLA, L. REV. 626 (1979) and citations therein, and see *infra*, note 115.

constituencies are the same, but the actions and attitudes of the representatives are not the same. There is not the slightest reason to suppose that the people are more accurately represented in the state legislatures than they are in Congress. Arithmetic suffices for this conclusion; since over half the American people live in nine states, a mere count of state legislatures is virtually meaningless. But even as to legislatures sitting in states containing a majority of the people, there is still the virtual certainty that different points of view and conceptions of office exist. As to issues of *national* consensus, the presumption has to be that Congress is the empowered voice.

The concept of "the same measure" is also problematic. The current death-penalty crisis illustrates this. Very considerably variant state statutes are a dubious source of evidence of consensus. For a highly simplified and schematized illustration, if a third of the states had no death penalty, another third had it for killing a policeman, and the remainder had it for murder by a lifer, there would be no majority consensus on the rightness of the penalty for anything. Since, moreover, the current controversy, as to constitutionality, is being fought on the issue of the adequacy of procedural due process in the system for picking people to die,[42] one could concede constitutional effect to state views only by holding that this value was at the mercy of the very entities the Fourteenth Amendment[43] was passed to restrain.

But the overriding point is that review of state actions for federal constitutionality—by far, I remind you, the most important kind of review—in no simple sense raises any questions at

42. See BLACK, CAPITAL PUNISHMENT: THE INEVITABILITY OF CAPRICE AND MISTAKE (1974).

43. The command that "No State shall . . . deprive any person of life . . . without due process of law," in the Fourteenth Admendment, hardly suggests that the state legislatures are to decide for themselves what "due process" may be.

all about conflict with democratic principles. The principles of democracy are no more at hazard when Connecticut is subjected to national law than they are when New Haven is subjected to Connecticut law. There is no strain on democratic principles in the fact that Connecticut's views, on federal constitutionality or on anything bearing on federal constitutionality, are of no weight in court. Aside from the unambiguous textual suggestions of the Supremacy Clause and the Fourteenth Amendment, the very nature of the case is that the national judicial power, interpreting the national Constitution, can be in relevant conflict—relevant, that is, to the problem of consonance with democratic assumptions—only with the national democratic branch. I am really quite surprised to note how very little attention, even yet, is given to this distinction, in the literature on judicial review and democracy.

Viewing as I do the matter of congressional power over the jurisdiction, original and appellate, of the federal courts,[44] the question I can ask myself, then, is whether a body of law— roughly, the constitutional guarantees of individual rights— which must be taken to state and implement a very high national interest, is suitable for enforcement by the federal courts, with the necessary interpretation, and with the immediate authority-impact of all other federal law, given the longstanding and, as I can honestly see it, the still-standing direction of the national legislature that this be done, and given the fact that no act of a state legislature, much less of any lower state official, can with any warrant be looked on as authoritative on constitutionality or on whatever value-judgments may be relevant to constitutionality.

I can't think that there is much doubt on this as to most constitutional law. The live question has to be whether the

---

44. *Supra*, pp. 37–39, and Introduction, *supra*, at pp. 18–19.

materials available as foundations for judicial judgment contain some concepts and terms so vague and ambiguous, so intractable to the normal intellectual processes of law, that a congressional command to apply them, and so, necessarily, to interpret them, must be *disobeyed*—on the Article III[45] ground that the judiciary has been commanded to perform a non-judicial function—as might be the case if the district judges were told to award $1,000, in reasonably lawful money of the United States, to every virtuous person who filed a nice-looking complaint, or to make sure, by the wielding of the mandatory and injunctive powers, that only reverend and discreet merchants were appointed to the Federal Trade Commission.[46]

I think we can go out at once to the personal-rights material, and take up the lines of decision that today most stirringly trouble the profession—those in which actions of the states claimed to be inimical to national constitutional rights are overturned on the basis of norms not literally expressed in the Constitution. A great part of the bad conscience of our time, concerning the problem of decision according to law, has to do with these cases.

The first thing I am going to do is to move that, having been proposed by the requisite majorities in Congress, and ratified by the requisite number of states, the Ninth Amendment to the Constitution of the United States at long last be adopted.

Let me read it out: "The enumeration in the Constitution, of certain rights, shall not be construed to deny or disparage others retained by the people."

I make this motion with the greater confidence because it

45. Article III of the Constitution establishes and distributes the "judicial power of the United States."

46. These would perhaps not be "judicial" functions, because the judges would have no intelligible standards by which to decide.

has already been seconded by a number of writers; a most able
seconding speech was made about a year ago by John Hart
Ely[47]—if indeed he did not himself make the motion, in which
case I cheerfully change my voice to that of a seconder.[48] The
urgent thing is that this adoption occur. We need the Ninth
Amendment, for the sake of honesty and for the sake of utility.

Some years ago, I suggested that one could easily ground
an "existence proof," as mathematicians call it, on the Ninth
Amendment, showing that it recognizes certain enforceable
rights other than those named elsewhere in the Constitution.[49]
Beyond any doubt, John Ely has given a new rigor to this
existence proof, and dealt conclusively with certain objections
to it. It is the constructive proof—the proof that leads to a
method of ascertaining what such rights are—that has seemed
to elude the grasp. This is because a general constructive proof
is very certainly impossible. Law is only by most inexact—
though sometimes enlightening—metaphor to be linked to

47. *Op. cit. supra*, note 17, pp. 33–41. John Ely's treatment seems to me
thoroughly to establish the propriety of resort to the Ninth Amendment as a fountain of
law, as against all the principal objections, but I cannot make out that he *proposes* this
course in so many words. So I will do so, to be sure the motion is before the house.

48. Actually, the parliamentary situation here is complicated. About ten years
ago, relying on the work of Prof. Norman Redlich and Prof. Mitchell Franklin, I
committed myself to the proposition that the Ninth Amendment should be looked on as
law, and that reasoning from analogy to express constitutional guarantees was a
warranted method of filling in its content. Black, *The Unfinished Business of the Warren
Court* (the Holmes Devise Lectures) 46 U. OF WASHINGTON L. REV. 3, 31–45 (1970).
As I read this article over now, I think I did not make positively enough the point that
analogy need not be the *only* method of giving the Ninth Amendment content.
Inferences from structure and relation (which I did mention and approve as warranted
grounds of law) might also be looked on as Ninth Amendment matter. Nor should other
methods be excluded.

(One should also mention PATTERSON, THE FORGOTTEN NINTH AMENDMENT
(1955).)

For an overseas view of the Ninth Amendment, see the judgment of Mr. Justice
Walsh in *McGee v. Atty. Gen.*, 1974 [Irish reports] 284, at p. 319, quoted in the new
O'Reilly and Redmond casebook (cited *infra* note 155) at p. 157.

49. In the piece just referred to, note 48.

mathematics. Law does not anywhere found legitimacy of claim or right only on rigorous methods rigidly limited as a class.

But is this more true of constructions under the Ninth Amendment than it is of constructions under any other method of deriving unnamed rights? The "due process" clause,[50] as a source of substantive rights, cannot even start to cover the range, without rudest violence to ordinary meaning—unless you take the words "of law" to mean "of law that is valid under the Constitution." This particular gloss is, I think, warrantable, even textually suggested by the Supremacy Clause,[51] which is more than you can say of the glosses put on "due process." It is no more than a curiosity of legal history that serious students and judges have been able to see in this latter phrase a *substantive* right to send your son to military school.[52] Necessity is the mother even of inventions that don't work. But the more plausible gloss on "law" does no more than start you all over again. "Equal protection," now at (or perhaps just past) the top of fashion, can never be more than a conduit, except as its placement in highly visible history ties it to racial matters, and to matters closely analogous to these.[53] (I will say, in parenthesis, that to me the most serious thing the "new" equal protection has done is, ever so slowly, but visibly in case and comment, to

50. U.S. CONSTITUTION, Amendment V, and Amendment XIV, Section 1, providing that no state "shall . . . deprive any person of life, liberty or property without due process of law. . . ."

51. Where supremacy of national laws is limited to those made "in pursuance" of the Constitution, U.S. CONSTITUTION, Article VI.

52. *Pierce v. Hill Military Academy*, 268 U.S. 510 (1925). This is a companion case to *Pierce v. Society of Sisters*, decided with it, but is more important theoretically than *Society of Sisters*, since that case could be viewed as involving, literally or by close analogy, the "free exercise of religion" clause, U.S. CONSTITUTION, Amendment I.

53. The Thirteenth, Fourteenth, and Fifteenth Amendments were in effect part of the settlement that ended a Civil War fought in some deep sense, as Lincoln saw, over race and racism. See also the next note.

change discrimination against blacks from a thing seen, in the noble 1880 opinion in *Strauder v. West Virginia*,[54] as being categorically forbidden, to a thing only "suspected," though with some depth, to be sure; that is what can happen when you take a term that stands in the chain of reasoning that supported the decision in a case like *Korematsu*[55]—the Japanese Exclusion case[56]—and try to make something good of it. The kiss of death never sweetens. This deplorable change, as to anti-black discrimination, may not work results as baneful as those of which it is theoretically capable. Let us pray.)

The Ninth Amendment, to be sure, similarly tells us nothing as to the nature of substantive rights outside the text, but, unlike "due process of law" and "equal protection of the laws," it irresistibly implies that they are there, and fairly implies that they are to be given effect, since it is vis-à-vis other rights that are to be given effect, that they are not to be taken to be "disparaged." A mere guide to the proper course to be taken by moral philosophy would, moreover, be an unbelievable exotic in a Constitution whose every sentence has operative legal effect.

What has all this Ninth Amendment talk to do with the states? Well, could you ever understand why Mr. Justice

54. 100 U.S. 303 (1880), holding it impermissible to try a black for murder before a jury that was made all-white by law. The aim of the Fourteenth Amendment, said the Court, was to strike down *"all possible legal discriminations"* against blacks.

55. *Korematsu v. U.S.*, 323 U.S. 214 (1944). Justice Black, writing for the Court, began his reasoning with the statement that ". . . all legal restrictions which curtail the civil rights of a single racial group are immediately *suspect*. This is not to say that all such restrictions are unconstitutional. It is to say that courts must subject them to the most *rigid scrutiny*." Put this language up against the language from Strauder, quoted in the immediately preceding note, and guess what happened to Korematsu. That's right. He went to jail for disobeying a law (or rather a General's order) that was racist in its terms. The words I have italicized in Black's formula became the fountainhead of the so-called "new" equal protection.

56. *Korematsu* has often been so called. Its right title would be wordier: "The American Citizens of Japanese Ancestry Concentration Camp Case."

Goldberg, in Griswold,[57] was so careful to disclaim the thought that the Ninth Amendment was good against the states?[58] I doubt he would have disclaimed thinking that the First Amendment was good against the states.[59] Either phrase is shorthand for a complicated formula. But if the second is not misleading, and not unacceptable, why should the first be?

Incorporation of the Ninth Amendment by the "privileges and immunities" clause of the Fourteenth, or by the clause of anybody's choice, ought to satisfy all parties in the "incorporation" controversy.[60] Hard-shelled "all and only" incorporators[61] must applaud, for there the Ninth Amendment is, in the magical black and white. Soft-shelled adepts of the "all and only those values which are fundamental" school cannot bridle; nothing can get into the Ninth Amendment on a technicality.

I shall therefore consistently, for what remains of these

57. *Griswold v. Connecticut*, 381 U.S. 479 (1965). This case struck down state laws forbidding the use of contraceptives. Since contraception is not mentioned in the Constitution, nor is there any general language which might be read, in any simple case, to "refer" to contraception, this case posed the problem (as the *Pierce* case had before, see note 52 *supra*) of the *unmentioned* right—the Ninth Amendment right, as I and others see the matter. See *supra*, at notes 47 and 48.

58. *Griswold v. Connecticut*, 381 U.S. 479, 492-3 (1965) (Goldberg, J. concurring). This passage well exhibits the intricate maneuvers into which one is forced by the feeling of reluctance to take the Ninth Amendment at its face value. Justice Goldberg works it around into a *confirmation* of the protection of unnamed rights under the word "liberty" in the due process clauses of the Fifth and Fourteenth Amendments. But why go around the barn that way?

59. As it has firmly been held to be, since *Gitlow v. New York*, 268 U.S. 652 (1925).

60. The controversy as to whether the Fourteenth Amendment, which lays generally worded restraints on the states, "incorporates by reference" the federal Bill of Rights. The short answer in the cases can now be seen to be that this "incorporation," whether or not so called, has very largely been effected, but that the Fourteenth Amendment includes other matter as well.

61. Those who believed every word of the national Bill of Rights was made applicable to the states by the Fourteenth Amendment, but that nothing else resulted from or was referred to by the Fourteenth Amendment. Justice Hugo Black was the chief of these. He did not, however, see anything much in the Ninth Amendment, probably because he didn't like it; see Ely, *op. cit. supra* note 17.

evenings and I hope for what remains of my life, use the expression "Ninth Amendment rights" to refer to those rights, privileges, and immunities not explicitly mentioned in the rest of the Constitution, whether applied against the national power or against the states. But, after all is said, if for some reason you do still prefer "equal protection" or "due process," there need be no substantive quarrel between us, ever. There is nothing placeable under either of those rubrics that cannot go under the Ninth Amendment, and nothing that can go under the Ninth Amendment that cannot be dragged in under one—or, if you try just a little harder, both—of these established incantations.

Let me say something about the relation to the Ninth Amendment of the analogic and structural modes of inference that I have written about in the past.[62] The short of it is—and this is one of the advantages of the Ninth Amendment approach—that every structural or analogic derivation of an unwritten personal right can be restated, with easy formal change, as a derivation of a Ninth Amendment right. No single such derivation gains or loses any intrinsic force by this restatement. It is conceivable that the intrinsic force of some derivations of this kind may strike some minds as insufficient for validating a claim not even generically mentioned, but as sufficient for validating a claim to inclusion within the class of rights referred to in the Ninth Amendment. This setting up of an atmosphere *hospitable* to the establishment of unnamed rights is a natural function of the Ninth Amendment's words. If I wanted to avoid it, I wouldn't know how.

The Ninth Amendment might take some time to work its clarifying way through the material, but it would be worth it. Take the First Amendment.[63] What if "Congress" did not

62. BLACK, STRUCTURE AND RELATIONSHIP IN CONSTITUTIONAL LAW (1969); also note 48, *supra*.

63. "Congress shall make no law . . . abridging the freedom of speech or of the press. . . ." U.S. CONSTITUTION, Amendment I.

"make" the "law" you are talking about, and it isn't even a law—say, a judge's overbroad gag order, or a lawless police chief's turning his dogs loose on demonstrators? Suppose the "people" didn't really "assemble,"[64] but peaceably corresponded, or peaceably sent in their dues. Going on, suppose— as in *Brown v. Maryland*[65]—the tax is not really on "imports,"[66] as commonly understood, but on the occupation of being an importer. Is it a "search" or a "seizure" when the police tap your telephone? Are the rules of double jeopardy applied to those trials that do not result in a judgment either of death or of mutilation because the chance of a long prison term is a "jeopardy of life," or because it is a "jeopardy of limb"? (Those are the two things the Fifth Amendment names.[67]) Since the phrase "bill of attainder" was used, in the days when the thing itself was used, to mean a legislative imposition of a death-sentence,[68] what is to be done about legislative provisions for the imprisonment of named persons?[69]

Oh, what a tangled web we weave! We have for a long time been fast-talking our way past road-blocks like these—or, more often and even worse, following a convention that one doesn't

---

64. The "right of the people peaceably to assemble" is named in Amendment I.

65. 12 Wheaton (U.S. Supreme Court) 419 (1827).

66. "No State shall, without the consent of Congress, lay any . . . duties on imports. . . ." U.S. CONSTITUTION, Article I, Section 10.

67. ". . . nor shall any person . . . for the same offense . . . be twice put in jeopardy of life or limb. . . ." The next self-proclaimed "strict constructionist" you run into, ask whether the cases are wrong that have applied this rule to "jeopardy" of being put in the penitentiary for a long time. (While you're holding on to his arm, ask him under which clause of the Constitution, "strictly constructed," Congress so stringently regulates the manufacture, possession, and sales of narcotics. Most self-styled "strict constructionists" are people who want the federal courts to lock dope peddlers up in federal penitentiaries, and throw away the key.)

68. STORY, COMMENTARIES ON THE CONSTITUTION §1338 (1833).

69. In fact, *all* of the applications of the "bill of attainder" prohibitions (in Article I, Sections 9 and 10) have concerned penalties less than death. Of course neither Congress nor any American state has ever tried to impose a death sentence by legislative fiat.

mention such things—that this kind of petty literalness is beneath dignity, except when we need it—or except when, on the other hand, it jumps up and bites us, as it did in *Paul v. Davis*,[70] a case I shall soon discuss (if "discussion" is not too weak a word). This sort of thing may be tolerable for some veterans who have acquired enough street sense to step around among these words, but I fear for our students. Where do they go next, from observing that it isn't the done thing to worry about whether a police chief is Congress, or whether "limb" means twenty years? They must early conclude that tactfully selective disregard of difficulty is the only way to a decent state of law—and that is the worst lesson we could teach them, because it undermines their professionalism, and leaves the decency of law naked to its enemies.

The Ninth Amendment does all that should be done about the gag order, the peaceable correspondence, the police dogs, all the rest; the low, easy road (though not the only road) into the Ninth Amendment would be a demonstration that the unnamed right is *closely analogous or functionally similar to a named right*.[71] You could talk about that very slowly and very thoroughly—just as you talk about the quite similar question whether a new case is like a cited precedent—and come through any kind of questioning you deserve to come through. Do you partly see why I think the Ninth Amendment has something to contribute to decision according to law?

There may be one practical substantive effect, and it is a good one, of the open Ninth Amendment approach. It may sometimes happen that one of the relatively narrow and specific Bill of Rights' guarantees is kept narrow because its very speci-

70. 424 U.S. 693 (1976). This case is treated *infra*, at pp. 50–54.

71. A fuller discussion, with references, is in my *The Unfinished Business of The Warren Court*, especially Part II, *The Unfinished Corpus Juris of Human Rights*, 46 WASHINGTON L. REV. 3, at pp. 31–45 (1970).

ficity isolates it methodologically from the broad and vague guarantees. I think here of the recent *Ingraham* case,[72] where it was held that the teachers could whip one junior high school student till hematomas formed, and he was laid up for eleven days, and could beat another one about the arms with a board, for all the Constitution cared. The "cruel and unusual punishments" claim was repelled on the ground that "punishment," in the Eighth Amendment,[73] refers only to punishment inflicted for crime. Even as a straight textual matter, this holding is hard to swallow. It takes a word of commonly understood meaning and cuts it down by construction, even though the word stands in a context where one would think expansive construction was the only right medicine; in a world where the maxims of construction travel in opposed pairs, how could it be right to choose the member of a pair that gives the more ample scope to cruel punishment? Every schoolboy knows that whipping is a punishment; what new lesson does he learn when told that if he had robbed a grocery store he couldn't be whipped, because that's a crime, but he can be whipped into eleven days out of school if (and I quote the statement of facts in *Ingraham*) "he was slow to respond to his teacher's instructions"?[74] Law, the government's omnipresent teaching assistant,[75] has here taught him something; I dislike thinking what.

But suppose one were marching down a methodologic road already well-traveled when one replied, to the contention that the Eighth Amendment has to do only with criminal punishment in the strictest sense, "Well, that sounds funny to me, but you may be right. But is not a child's claim against cruel

72. 430 U.S. 651 (1977).
73. U.S. CONSTITUTION, Amendment VIII.
74. 430 U.S. 651, 657 (1977).
75. "Our Government is the potent, the omnipresent teacher." Mr. Justice Brandeis, dissenting in *Olmstead v. U.S.*, 277 U.S. 438 (1928).

punishment in school—sorry, cruel chastisement—so close to the Eighth Amendment, in equity and ethical foundation, that the present claim has to be validated under the Ninth Amendment?" This question does not answer itself. But it is a question addressed entirely to the *rationality* of a distinction. Could the four *Ingraham* dissenters perhaps have picked up one more vote and the law so have taught that boy a different lesson, if the question had been altogether of that form?

Indeed, the *Ingraham* style of narrowing is a threat even to the range of the supposedly more open-textured clauses, such as, *par excellence*, the "due process" clause. In the 1976 *Paul v. Davis* decision, to which I have briefly alluded,[76] it appeared that the police, on the basis of a mere *charge* of shoplifting—a charge shortly afterward dismissed—put the plaintiff's name and picture on a widely distributed flyer listing "active shop-lifters." The Court found no constitutional invasion in this profoundly injurious official action by public officials—on the ground, forsooth, that "reputation," was not "liberty" or "property." Mr. Justice Brennan's dissent was uphill labor, because reputation, colloquially, probably is not usually referred to as "liberty" or "property"—though one would think that a legal system that can treat infringements of a common-law copyright in personal letters as a property invasion,[77] or compensate the frightening of chickens as a "taking" of property,[78] would not be quite so firmly tied down by colloquial usage. A state of the law which makes that majority holding and opinion possible, and the dissent a labor, is a state in which, *pro tanto*, irrationality rules—and in which, I might add, "principle" plays no part.

We are sometimes stuck with such a state of the law. But we are not stuck here. There is the Ninth Amendment, not only

---

76. See note 70 above.
77. *Gee v. Pritchard*, 2 Swanst. 402, 36 English Reprint 670 (1818).
78. *U.S. v. Causby*, 328 U.S. (1946).

authorizing but obliging us to ask, "Is the interest in not being officially branded as an active criminal not an interest worthy of protection in any constitutional system that protects people from having a sack of potatoes seized without process of law?" I commend this *Paul* case to you as antidote for any thought that textualism is allied to rationality, while the Ninth Amendment approach is not. Strongly on the contrary, the Ninth Amendment, perhaps above its other merits, makes possible fully rational discourse in the formation of personal rights law, *toward the construction of a coherent system*. It is the highest wisdom of any legal order—the most sternly requisite task of technical acumen—to seek and to cleave unto any resource that opens up that possibility to the art of law. In this transcendent sense, the Ninth Amendment could be the gate to the best kind we can attain of decision according to law. When technique can bring us to this point, the string and the bow will be readied for such coaction as can be in the cities of earth. The drive for adoption of the Ninth Amendment is a quest after something very precious.

To revert to the principal question: Is there, then, something inherently unjudicial in the filling out of the open texture of the Ninth Amendment with a finding of rights in some way validated for inclusion, though not specifically named anywhere else in the Constitution—insofar as this work is a part of the congressionally commanded work of applying the Constitution to the states? My instinct on this, as pretty much always, is to go for examples, and so to try to get the range of problematic material. Necessary caution makes me say that there need be no *general* answer as to how one tells whether the mode of derivation of what I will call "Ninth Amendment" rights is marked by the quality of lawfulness, because there need not be, and is not, a single method generally commanded. On the other hand, I trust there is no one here who thinks that the adoption of the

Ninth Amendment would imply acceptance of any argument proferred as a Ninth Amendment argument. But that is about what some writers seem to have thought, *mutatis mutandis*, about my "structure and relationship"[79] suggestions, so I explicitly point out that each single Ninth Amendment argument stands on its own. The imaginativeness of lawyers being what it is, I would expect most such arguments to fail.

Now the range I will go through does no more than point to a few terms in a series which we have no reason to think has only a *numerus clausus* of terms.

And I must mention a problem of presentation. As to all the examples that follow, it is my own view that the questions ought to be seen as Ninth Amendment questions—questions as to the need for the Ninth Amendment, questions as to the rightness of finding the asserted claim in the Ninth Amendment, made to run against the states by the Fourteenth. The Court, on the other hand, has seen these questions as "due process" and "equal protection" questions. I shall try to pick my way through this difficulty with as little stumbling, or causing to stumble, as possible.

First there is the case that would use the Ninth Amendment only as a textual conduit for the validation of an interest or claim that would have been validated without any such textual support. One of the most puzzling of recent cases is *Police Department of Chicago v. Mosley,*[80] a picketing case, wherein the Court, after reciting the settled and evidently correct rule, altogether sufficient for decision, that "government has no power [under the First Amendment] to restrict expression because of its message," then shifts, with no perceptible gain in power-ratio, into the equal protection gear.[81] The suggestion

79. See *supra*, note 62.
80. 408 U.S. 92 (1972).
81. 408 U.S. at 96, 101.

of such a shift is that something was added at this point; I cannot begin to guess what that was. Ninth Amendment thinking would have nothing to add here—just as "equal protection" thinking had nothing to add. (Though I should say that it takes functional-similarity reasoning, to which the Ninth Amendment offers textual hospitality, to cover picketing with the immunities of either "speech" or "press.")

Much the same things are true, I should suppose, of *Shapiro v. Thompson*,[82] which struck down residency requirements for welfare eligibility—and all the other cases striking down impediments on free movement, including transfer of residence, within the United States. The constitutional principle invoked in *Shapiro* is venerable and protean, moving from text to text, and quite comfortable without a text to hide under, in *Crandall v. Nevada*,[83] and I believe in *United States v. Guest*,[84] where Mr. Justice Stewart suggests that the right was not "explicitly" mentioned in the Constitution because it was "conceived . . . to be a necessary concomitant of the stronger Union the Constitution created."[85] (The only puzzlement in that passage comes from the fact that the weaker Union the Constitution replaced *did* explicitly provide for a right to travel, in Article IV of the Articles of Confederation—which in turn makes it, I should say, certain that Article IV of the Constitution, standing in a document that is to form "a more perfect Union," is to be heard, at least in its pristine state, unembarrassed by confusing and enfeebling interpretation, as *mentioning*, as one of the mentioned privileges, the privilege of going where all the other privileges and immunities were.)

The equal protection clause, then, says the same thing as

82. 394 U.S. 618 (1969).
83. 6 Wallace 35 (U.S. Supreme Court, 1867).
84. 383 U.S. 745 (1966).
85. 383 U.S. at p. 758.

Crandall v. Nevada, Edwards v. California,[86] *United States v. Guest,* probably the Article IV privileges and immunities clause, and (as to *Mosley*) the First Amendment at its core. These cases show that sometimes the whole "fundamental interest" and "suspect classification" and "strict scrutiny" business may be a fifth wheel—made out of any material you like, since it is to bear no weight. Far from presenting any problem as to derivation from law, the *Shapiro* and *Mosley* cases are high and dry in this regard, and only bemuse by their election to take off into the equal protection empyrean.

If you will indulge me, let us take up in more detail another of the decisional lines lately dominated by the "new" equal protection.

There are two ways to search for the law regarding discriminations against lawfully resident aliens.

One is to inquire whether alienage is a "suspect" classification, by seeking in alienage abstract characteristics found in other "suspect" classifications—such as its falling within the borders of the famous 1938 Carolene Products footnote,[87]

86. 314 U.S. 160 (1941). This case held that the clause giving Congress power "to regulate commerce among the several states" contained the implication that California was forbidden to make it a crime to bring into the state "any indigent person . . . not a resident of the State. . . ." Edwards had brought in his down-on-his-luck brother-in-law. That this negative inference could be drawn, from a clause that seems merely to empower Congress, is doubly questionable. Besides the general inference of state lack of power from the existence of (unexercised) congressional power, one must treat this family matter as "commerce." Besides that, the disenablement of California in this matter might seem to imply that *Congress* could make it a crime to take poor folks across a state line. If this inference is not to be drawn, it must be because of some express or implied *general prohibition* against such a law—a prohibition that would rest at least as clearly on California as on Congress.

87. In this (1938) footnote, Chief Justice Stone, after holding in the case actually before him that total irrationality of the law under review was necessary for a holding of unconstitutionality of an economic regulation, suggested that some other cases might not require quite so exacting a standard: "There may be narrower scope for operation of the presumption of constitutionality when legislation appears on its face to be within a specific prohibition of the Constitution, such as those of the first ten Amendments,

where Mr. Justice Stone suggested the appropriateness of special judicial solicitude for discrete and insular minorities.

The other comes out with thoughts like these: The decision to admit aliens to residence in the United States is a national decision, committed to Congress. State laws and regulations making residence difficult for aliens limit the effect of the national decision, which must be assumed to have a national purpose—whether that purpose be economic, moral, or something else. The general conclusion would be that such state laws are invalid, under the eternally productive principle of *McCulloch v. Maryland*. [88] This line of thought is supported by the consideration that the status of aliens is a sensitive matter in foreign affairs—a subject from which the states are explicitly excluded in part, and in part excluded by long-accepted implications. [89]

But such a line of general reasoning may admit of historical or other well-grounded exceptions. The Constitution, at several points, admits alienage as a reasonable ground for exclusion from national public office; [90] it would be anomalous to

which are deemed equally specific when held to be embraced within the Fourteenth. . . .

It is unnecessary to consider now whether legislation which restricts those political processes which can ordinarily be expected to bring about repeal of undesirable legislation, is to be subjected to more exacting judicial scrutiny under the general prohibitions of the Fourteenth Amendment than are most other types of legislation. . . .

"Nor need we enquire whether similar considerations enter into the review of statutes directed at particular religious or racial minorities. Whether prejudice against discrete and insular minorities may be a special condition, which tends seriously to curtail the operation of those political processes ordinarily to be relied upon to protect minorities, and which may call for a correspondingly more searching judicial inquiry. . . ."—*United States v. Carolene Products Co.*, 304 U.S. 144 (1938), footnote 4.

88. 4 Wheaton 316 (U.S. Supreme Court, 1819).

89. See my STRUCTURE AND RELATIONSHIP IN CONSTITUTIONAL LAW, pp. 64–65 (1969).

90. This is true of all national elective office: U.S. CONSTITUTION, Article I, Section 2 (Congressman); *ib.* Section 3 (Senators); *ib*, Article II, Section 1 (President).

find, in the same Constitution, that one must have been a
citizen of the United States for seven years in order to be a
Congressman, but need not be a citizen in order to be governor
of a state. State legislatures and executive and judicial officers
must, moreover, take an oath to support the Constitution of the
United States, by explicit provision of Article VI. The propriety
of citizenship as a qualification for voting seems to be recognized, as assumed background, in no less than four and argu-
ably five amendments to the Constitution, three of them
ratified in this century, and one within the last decade.[91] The
result would seem to be that the states may make alienage a
disqualifying circumstance for voting or for holding political
office, but may not impose onerous terms on aliens as such,
with respect to their mode of life, mobility, employment, and
similar matters. There will be penumbral cases—the recent
case about aliens as policemen[92] is perhaps such a case, though
I would not have solved it as the Court did—and there may be
quite large problems we have not yet thought about; we will take
them up as we reach them. One of them seems to have been
reached just yesterday,[93] in the Supreme Court, where it was
held that alienage may permissibly be made a disqualification
for teaching school. I have not had opportunity to read or
consider the opinions, but my first impression is that this
decision is not right.[94]

91. Amendments as follows: XIV, Section 2 (1868); XV, Section 1 (1870); XIX
(1919); XXIV, Section 1 (1964); XXVI, Section 1 (1971).

92. *Foley v. Connelie*, 435 U.S. 291 (1978). The Court held that a state may
exclude aliens from eligibility to become policemen.

93. *Ambach v. Norwick*, U.S., 99 S. Ct. 1589 (1979). The judgment was handed
down April 17, 1979, the date of the first of the Holmes Lectures on which this book is
based. A constitutional law academic is part a journalist *maugré lui!*

94. I continue in this belief. Teaching school is not an occupation comparable to
the policy-forming offices for which aliens are made ineligible by the Constitution.
There is, I think, no sufficient reason for making this kind of employment an exception
to the general rule that the Congress, by ordaining that an alien may live among us, has
implicitly ordained that that alien shall not be barred by state law from making a living at
a lawful calling.

Congress is of course not bound by these considerations, but is bound by the federal Bill of Rights, including the Ninth Amendment. Aliens not only are "persons" for purposes of construing the Bill of Rights—a plain-meaning judgment—but also are part of "the People" for the same purpose. This conclusion is in harmony with the Article I rules for enumeration as a basis for dividing representative among the states. It is a settled expectation that many aliens are to become citizens; their children born here are citizens at birth.[95] The fact that aliens do not vote cannot of itself be decisive on the question of their being part of the people, because when the words were used in the Bill of Rights, women, free blacks, and in some states persons without property, were generally excluded from voting. Children still are, everywhere.

Still, there may be regulations, not violating any of the rights named in, or fairly inferrible from, the Bill of Rights, that Congress may make, in exercise of that very power over aliens, and the terms of their residency, which generally preempts state power. There is some room for the consideration that Congress's power to admit or not to admit may imply the power to admit on conditions. Moreover, this is not an area in which the national power is wielded in the same way and over the same subjects as are dealt with by the states;[96] this is a distinctively national subject. Some of the Bill of Rights' provisions may indeed, in the very nature of the case, not work out the same for aliens as for citizens. Banishment, for example, is a cruel and unusual punishment for citizens,[97] but whatever tenure aliens may have in resident status would have to be worked out on different lines. The content of the Ninth Amendment is to be constructed by reasoned operations, and no one can be sure in advance that such operations will always lead to the same results

95. Amendment XIV, Section I.
96. See *infra* at p. 77.
97. *Trop v. Dulles*, 356 U.S. 86 (1958).

in the respective cases of aliens and citizens; the banishment distinction may have a structural counterpart in Ninth Amendment law.

But the power to effect discriminations against aliens, even at the national level, is part of Congress's power, and on so sensitive a matter, cutting so deep into the lives of people, Congress itself should have to make a readable judgment that such discrimination is necessary. The federal bureaucracy should not be held empowered to do so under broad and blind delegations.[98]

In all this there may be room for some independent presidential action, and for congressional delegation to the president under reasonably clear standards, in view of possible connections with foreign affairs and military security.

Now that took a long time. I did it not because I wanted to give you a short course in the constitutional law of alienage. I would be a laughably poor instructor for such a course; I am not at all sure that all the conclusions are right. Certainly not all of them are supported by decisional law, though some venerable cases, like *Truax v. Raich*,[99] stand as marks of this line of

98. An alternative, often available, would be a judicial refusal to interpret broad and blind delegations as granting power to administrators to sail close to the wind of constitutional values. Thus, in *Kent v. Dulles*, 357 U.S. 116 (1958), the Court held that language of a thoroughly general, literal tenor was not to be read as conferring, on the secretary of state, authority to deny a passport to one who refused to take an oath as to whether he was or had ever been a Communist.

99. 239 U.S. 33 (1915). Of a state statute limiting the percentage of an employer's workforce that could be aliens, the Court said:

The authority to control immigration—to admit or exclude aliens—is vested solely in the Federal Government. Fong Yue Ting v. United States, 149 U.S. 698, 713. The assertion of an authority to deny to aliens the opportunity of earning a livelihood when lawfully admitted to the State would be tantamount to the assertion of the right to deny them entrance and abode, for in ordinary cases they cannot live where they cannot work. And, if such a policy were permissible, the practical result would be that those lawfully admitted to the country under the authority of the acts of Congress, instead of enjoying a substantial sense and in their full scope the privileges conferred by the admission, would be segregated in such of the States as chose to offer hospitality.—239 U.S. at 42.

thought's not being purely imaginary. I am interested here only in illustrating one way of thinking about law.

Maybe the choice between that way of thinking and the way of thinking exemplified by the "new" equal protection analysis is to some degree personal and temperamental. I confess I do like the sound of one mode better than the other. I very much dislike the concept of "suspicion" of the work of the legislative branch, as a regular tool of constitutional analysis, just as I dislike the now hackneyed phrase "to pass muster," with its overtones of military inspection by a superior officer, to apply to that work. I don't like the use of the concept of "overwhelming" state interest when you mean that no state interest will do. I don't like the elevation of the Carolene Products footnote[100] to super-constitutional status when it works for you, and its disregard when you get to discrimination against women, where its application would be laughable. But let me be a little more detailed about the rational grounds, as I sense them, of my strong preference for the alternative to the "new" equal protection thought as applied to aliens.

I prefer it, chiefly and strongly, because of a characteristic that may put others off: *It is all about aliens.* It attempts to make rational ties between the constitutional law of aliens and other positive legal institutions. It does not, needlessly and without warrant, store up trouble for another day. For example, it puts the voting-officeholding exception on positive grounds having to do with nothing but alienage;[101] it neither seeks nor sets in place any general rules, dangerous as these would be, about the abstract characteristics a class must have in order to make its exclusion from political office permissible. Some people seem

100. See *supra*, note 87.

101. It is to be observed that this mode of thought would have drawn a reasonably clear limitation of the "office-holding" exception, confining it to state offices of an importance comparable to the ones named in the Constitution. Policemen and school-teachers would not have been among these; see *supra* at notes 92–94.

to think such general formulae should be essayed as often as possible; I think they should be constructed as rarely as possible.

On the other hand, the use of this lower-abstraction, single-problem, structural reasoning gives you everything you are going to get, or ought to get, as to alienage. You can call alienage a "suspect classification," and call voting a "fundamental right," but you are going to have to let the states exclude aliens from voting. In the frame of thought that has been traditional for about the last four thousand days, you'll have to find an "overwhelming" state interest in this step. Since some states did let some aliens vote up into the twenties of this century, and since the overwhelming interest in not letting them vote is hard to pin down and put a name to, you'll have to recede to some lower level of so-called analysis—to medium scrutiny, perhaps. One begins to think of the grades of fault: culpa levissima, culpa levis, culpa simpliciter, culpa gravis, and culpa gravissima, I think they were. Or something like that. Don't you remember how useful they turned out to be?

But there is more than just fun here; there is great danger. In a saying both observant and prophetic, Professor Cox remarked a few years ago that the idea of equality is not easily cabined.[102] But it is easily diluted, distorted, and balkanized. What is to happen to the idea of equality when aliens are declared equal—subject of course to the reservations that the states may bar them from political participation, while Congress may have them register once a year and may, at least for good cause shown, deport them? Is everybody who is "equal" going to be just that "equal"? Or, in one of life's infinitely various imitations of art, are we coming up to 1984 with some equal people more equal than others?

---

102. "Once loosed, the idea of Equality is not easily cabined." Cox, *The Supreme Court, 1965 Term. Foreword: Constitutional Ajudication and the Promotion of Human Rights*, 80 HARVARD L. REV. 91 (1966).

I have concluded that it will be best to take up the problem of discrimination against women just a little further along, where it connects with federal power, and now to give a slightly postdated check, for payment, so far as my means suffice, in a few minutes. I will just say, by way of anticipation, that to me the immunity from diminishment of rights, on the ground that one is a woman, while it is not a creation of law entirely outside Ninth Amendment territory, as are the immunities in *Shapiro* and *Mosley*, can assert firm and positively establishable claims to being a right under the Ninth Amendment—and I am not going to base my conclusion on anything at all about the English-speaking peoples or rights dear to the heart of civilized (if you will pardon the irony of the cliché) man, but rather on rational ties to other parts of the constitutional-law system, matters of record rather than matters of philosophy.

Let me pass on to the final question as to federal-on-state review—one of great intricacy and of high interest. What of the thing I could call the pure Ninth Amendment case, wherein the value of the asserted interest and the unacceptability of its wounding are pronounced on by the Court without the help of a declaration in the Constitution, an analogy from the Constitution, a structural implication from the Constitution, or matter of record as to national judgment?

I would bring this inquiry down closer to political earth by noticing that (with the very important exception of the abortion cases) these pure Ninth Amendment decisions, as I call them, though far from trivial in importance, still have not turned out to be of a practical and political interest proportioned to their very high intricacy. Very few widely controversial decisions have involved judicial discernment of fundamental interests even so much as questionable. There was no problem about the established title to fundamentalness of the right of blacks to immunity from discrimination based on their being black, or of

the claim to fair procedures in criminal law enforcement, or of
the claim to immunity from religious coercion or pressure in
public school. These interests are fundamental because they are
given that character by the written Constitution. The more
permissive obscenity decisions[103] were wrong, if at all, not
because they rested on an intuition of fundamentalness in pais,
but because they wrongly bounded a named fundamental right.
As to the cases on legislative district size, I could not go along
with some of the more advanced of these decisions, and (after
strong "equal protection" misgivings expressed as early as
1967)[104] I now agree with my colleague Robert Bork that all the
state-legislature cases should have been put on the "guarantee
clause."[105] Since election "by the people" is a defining character of eighteenth-century "republicanism," this step would have
resulted in the state cases' being off the same bolt of cloth as
Wesberry v. Sanders,[106] where the Article I "by the People"
requirement was the source of decision for congressional districting. But it could hardly have occurred to the mind that the
discernment of fundamentalness in the voting right, in the
United States of all places, had to implicate natural law, or
personal predilection of the judges. The "Impeach Warren"
bumper stickers came into flower, then, not because the Court,
in its more bitterly controversial cases, rested judgment on
intuitions about the finest traditions of Western culture, or
anything of the sort. In these politically explosive cases, the
Court was confined from molar to at least relatively molecular
motions—to questions about the scope of interests possessing

103. E.g., *Jenkins v. Georgia,* 418 U.S. 153 (1974).
104. See my *Representation in Law and Equity,* in (Pennock and Chapman, eds.)
REPRESENTATION (1968).
105. Bork, *Neutral Principles and Some First Amendment Problems,* 47 INDIANA
L. J. 1, 19 (1971). I guess I ought to add that I agree only with this single general
substitution. (Bork does not develop the link with congressional districting cases.)
106. 376 U.S. 1 (1964).

solidly attested fundamental character, and about suitable remedies.

Now beyond such cases, and beyond the cases concerning travel, alienage, and of all things free speech, and beyond discriminations against women—to which my postdated check will very soon be due—where has the Court actually gone? There's a mirage here, a shimmering mirage of commentary, of explanation along philosophic lines. But what is being explained?

In overwhelming preponderance, what is being explained is a special guarding of the intimacies and autonomies of pro-creative and family life. That is *Skinner,*[107] *Pierce v. Society of Sisters,*[108] and, more clearly, the other *Pierce* case,[109] where the plaintiff was a military school, and no religion issue confused the parental issue. That was *Griswold* and *Roe v. Wade.*[110] *Moore v. City of East Cleveland,*[111] holding that a grandmother cannot be prevented by law from having her ten-year-old or-phaned grandson live with her, is within this category. (The reading of that case convinced me that it is very difficult to put to a class an imaginary case that is more grotesque than real cases. The parade of horribles goes right through downtown East Cleveland.)

Do you want me to stand up here and make the case for regarding as "fundamental" the interest in privacy and au-tonomy as respects the married life, the relations of children,

107. *Skinner v. Oklahoma,* 316 U.S. 535 (1942), holding invalid a state law commanding sterilization of some (but not all) thrice-convicted felons.
108. 268 U.S. 510 (1925), striking down, at the suit of a Catholic parochial school, a law requiring attendance of all children at public schools.
109. *Pierce v. Hills Brothers,* 268 U.S. 510 (1925).
110. *Griswold v. Connecticut,* 381 U.S. 479 (1965), was the leading case in-validating state laws prohibiting contraception, see above, notes 57 and 58. *Roe v. Wade,* 410 U.S. 113 (1973), was the leading case invalidating state laws prohibiting abortion.
111. 431 U.S. 949 (1977).

parents, and even grandparents, the chance and choice to have a child? Think before you answer by acclamation or by the gesture of thumbs up, because we would be here long into the chilly spring night. I couldn't stop with the English-speaking peoples, but would have to go back before there was an English language, back to the primitive Germanic-speaking peoples, the primitive Indo-Hittite-speaking peoples, the speakers of languages spoken before there was a Britain separated from the European mainland. It would be quite arbitrary to stop with Western civilization; Africa, Asia, both Americas before Columbus must be heard from.

If the pure Ninth Amendment is to contain anything beyond material validated by strong structural implication or strong analogy from other parts of the Constitution or by congressional declarations of great solemnity, then there is nothing more eligible for inclusion than protection of what I will call, meaning to use the term in a wide sense, the marriage and parent-child interest. I think we are warranted, by the Ninth Amendment, in acting as if, in the First Amendment, a semicolon were put after "grievances," followed by the words "or abridging the privacies and freedoms of matrimonial, parental and family life." You might say a leap is taken. But can you think of it as a leap in the dark?

The working out of such a principle of protection does entail very many leaps in the dusk, at least, but these are much shorter leaps—maybe even just long steps, such as courts always must take when they have to work a principle into the life of a time and place. It should be well-pondered that the alternative to taking them, and so to running the chance that not every one of them is right, is to give up the thought of implementing the principle at all.

It should be pondered, too, that this alternative is a constant in all law, marking decidedly—and this should be well-noted—the most textual of textualism. It is impossible even to begin talking about whether the textually explicit protection of speech and press is an "absolute" until you have left in the rear the perhaps tacit resolutions of such questions as the fraud question, the trade-secrets question, the copyright question, the malicious personal slander question, the noise question, the counterfeit ten-dollar-bill question, the trademark and unfair competition question, the ugly-billboard question, the conspiracy question, the incitement-to-murder question, the malpractice question, the contract-not-to-publish question, and so on. Just in this way, acceptance of the principle of family and parent-child autonomy would be the beginning of a process of inclusion and exclusion, based very much on what is thought or known about expectations and patterns within our society. Remember that we are still not at the end of defining the relations of freedom of speech to the interest in not being defamed.[112]

Now what real flights has the Court taken, outside the field of family, in the wide sense?

The holdings scatter, past this point. There is a right to teach a foreign language, at least functionally connectable with the rights of free expression, if not actually subsumable thereunder.[113] There is a wavering and doubtful immunity from discrimination on the ground of illegitimacy.[114] I dare say I am missing some.

It doesn't make any difference, for our present purposes, what you and I think of any of these cases. If we disagreed, that

112. *New York Times v. Sullivan,* 376 U.S. 254 (1964); *Gertz v. Robert Welch, Inc.,* 418 U.S. 323; *Herbert v. Lando,* 441 U.S. 153 (1979).

113. *Meyer v. Nebraska,* 262 U.S. 390 (1923).

114. The holdings pendulate from year to year. *Levy v. Louisiana,* 391 U.S. 68 (1968); *Labine v. Vincent,* 401 U.S. 532 (1971); *Weber v. Aetna Casualty and Surety Co.,* 406 U.S. 164 (1972); *Mathews v. Lucas,* 427 U.S. 495 (1976); *Trimble v. Gordon,* 430 U.S. 762 (1977); *Lalli v. Lalli,* 439 U.S. (1978).

would only show that disagreement is possible over a Ninth Amendment question, as it is possible over the question of the meaning of the seemingly plain words, "a Convention for proposing Amendments,"[115]

I ought to say generally (before leaving the state-law material) that, while my own conclusions quite clearly appear, my only committed purpose, just now, is to show that this material can be justified, if not as being in every case right, at least as being within the range of lawful decision. No legal argument can be entirely demonstrative; this fact, with which thought about law must start, implies that even decisions with which one does not agree may be taken "according to law."

Before we reach the pure *Marbury v. Madison*[116] area, we need to take careful note of an intermediate and very important category—one not covered by the Thayer-Holmes dichotomy, and possibly not often separated out for attention: the case of judicial review of federal action other than Acts of Congress. This category has a wide range—all the way from the president,[117] down to collectors of customs,[118] and back up to the House of Representatives, as a part but not the whole of Congress.[119] The distinguishing feature of all such cases is that the

115. U.S. CONSTITUTION, Article V. For recent glimpses at this decades-long controversy, see Dellinger, *The Recurring Question of the "Limited" Constitutional Convention*, 88 Yale L. J. 1623 (1979); Van Alstyne, *Does Article V Restrict the States to Calling Unlimited Conventions Only?* 1978 DUKE L. J. 1295 (1978); and my own *Amendment by National Constitutional Convention: A Letter to A Senator*, 32 OKLA. L. REV. 626 (1979), citing earlier articles. Compare *supra*, note 41.

116. Those cases, that is to say, that concern the invalidation, by the Court, of an *Act of Congress*. See *supra* at note 31.

117. *Youngstown Sheet and Tube Co. v. Sawyer* (The Steel Seizure Case), 343 U.S. 579 (1952).

118. *U.S. v. Wong Kim Ark* 169 U.S. 649 (1898).

119. *Powell v. McCormack*, 395 U.S. 486 (1969). Much of the commentary on this case treats it as a conflict between the Court and "Congress." But neither the Senate nor the president had spoken even informally in the case; such a case, while involving important intergovernmental conflict, is not one of judicial conflict with "Congress."

full national political branch had not recorded its conviction either of the practical wisdom or of the constitutionality of the reviewed measure.

The most interesting thing here is the diversity of ways in which the actual decisions taken relate to congressional power. I can do no more than mention a few principal divisions.

There is no conflict at all with any non-judicial authority when the appellate court reviews the action of the federal judge who, without statutory direction, admits evidence claimed to be inadmissible under the Constitution.

The presidential action taken without claim even of general delegation from Congress—as in the *Youngstown Steel* case,[120] *ex parte Milligan*,[121] the *Prize* cases[122]—raises questions of its own. But obviously there was no *Marbury v. Madison* problem in the *Youngstown Steel* case, or in any cases of that form.

But most federal officials act under some kind of a delegation of power from Congress, proximate or remote, standard-bound or to all practical purposes standardless. The needful caution here is that the traceability of the power to Congress, by ascent of the delegation ladder, does not imply factually, and should therefore not be taken to imply legally, that Congress has made the crucial judgment of constitutionality, or the crucial prudential judgment of propriety or necesity. There is no room here for "deeming."

I shall have to pass on, intending, by what I have just said, only to alert you to the elusiveness of congressional implication in anything but an Act or Resolution of Congress. But, be it noticed, we have here an important class of reviewing

120. *Supra* note 117.

121. 4 Wallace (71 U.S.) 2 (1867).

122. 2 Black 635 (U.S. Supreme Court, 1863). In a 5-4 decision, the Court upheld the 1861 declaration, by Abraham Lincoln, of the blockade against Southern ports.

actions—not as dominatingly vast, to be sure, as the federal-on-state class, but, like the latter, in no way implicating the philosophy or the political problems of *Marbury v. Madison*. Most important, the "clash with democracy" problem occurs, if at all, only in a highly attenuated form.

When we turn to judicial review of Acts of Congress, let me once again be concrete about the exercise of that function in recent decades. The invalidating actions taken within the last forty-two-years, with respect to Acts of Congress, concern small or middle-sized matters politically, and the intellectual problems, the problems of method, seem definitely to be on a smaller scale than in some of the federal-on-state lines. Several cases concern the irrationality of particular presumptions in criminal cases[123]—just the sort of thing judges have for centuries pronounced on at common law. A few others deal with the forbidden self-incrimination inhering in certain required disclosures.[124] One extends the well-established right to travel[125] to foreign travel. Another handful ring the changes on the idea that United States citizenship may not be taken away as a penalty.[126] Some others, one by one, rest on narrow holdings on particular provisions, like the *Lovett* case finding a bill of attainder in an Act declaring the ineligibility of three named persons to be paid for federal employment.[127] One, the *Jackson* case, struck down a provision seen as impairing the jury-trial right.[128] Several work out the implications of the evidently

123. *Tot v. U.S.*, 319 U.S. 463 (1943); *U.S. v. Romano*, 382 U.S. 136 (1955); *Leary v. U.S.*, 395 U.S. 6 (1969).

124. *Albertson v. Subversive Activities Control Board*, 382 U.S. 70 (1965); *Marchetti v. U.S.*, 390 U.S. 39 (1968); *Leary v. U.S.*, 395 U.S. 6 (1969).

125. *Aptheker v. Secy of State*, 378 U.S. 500 (1964).

126. *Trop v. Dulles*, 356 U.S. 86 (1958); *Kennedy v. Mendoza-Martinez*, 372 U.S. 144 (1963); cf. *Afroyim v. Rusk*, 387 U.S. 253 (1967).

127. *U.S. v. Lovett*, 328 U.S. 303 (1946).

128. *U.S. v. Jackson*, 390 U.S. 570 (1968); see also *Pope v. U.S.*, 392 U.S. 651 (1968).

sensible (and quite particularized) idea that court-martial jurisdiction is to be *strictissimi juris*. [129] I would point out that none
of these cases could have involved any very large general principles. Going on, there are perhaps half a dozen fairly narrow
holdings on free utterance, [130] and one such holding on the
establishment clause. [131] Even *Buckley v. Valeo* [132] does not
struggle with ultimate questions of value; it takes the free-
utterance value as given (how not?) and tries to work out the
problems arising from the connection of contribution and ex-
penditure with utterance. *National League of Cities v. Usery* [133]
in no way brings in questions about the values of civilization, or
the fundamentalness of human interests. The one case of
federal-on-federal review dealing with illegitimacy, *Jímenez v.
Weinberger*, [134] explicitly declines to decide whether illegitimacy is a "so-called 'suspect' classification," and decides the
case on the basis of a discerned irrationality in a scheme for
distinguishing between two different classes of illegitimates.

I have no wish to minimize these cases; the very fact that
the Court is policing these matters—and so showing itself ready
to police other matters—is of large significance. But if we are
looking—and remember, we are talking about forty-two years,
including years of all-time maximum judicial questing—for a

129. *U.S.* ex rel. *Toth v. Quarles*, 350 U.S. 11 (1955); *Reed v. Covert*, 354 U.S.
1 (1957); *Kinsella v. U.S.*, 361 U.S. 234 (1960); *Grisham v. Hagen*, 361 U.S. 278
(1960); *O'Callahan v. Parker*, 395 U.S. 258 (1969).

130. *Lamont v. Postmaster General*, 381 U.S. 301 (1965); *U.S. v. Brown*, 381
U.S. 437 (1965); *U.S. v. Robel*, 389 U.S. 258 (1967); *Schacht v. U.S.*, 398 U.S. 58
(1970); *Blount v. Rizzi*, 400 U.S. 410 (1971); *Buckley v. Valeo*, 424 U.S. 1 (1976).

131. *Tilton v. Richardson*, 403 U.S. 672 (1971).

132. Cited in note 130 above. The case concerned permissibility of certain
regulations of campaign contributions and expenditures.

133. 426 U.S. 833 (1976), holding that the application of federal wages-and-
hours standards to state-government employees violated the "reserved rights" of the
states.

134. 417 U.S. 628 (1974), invalidating a Social Security Act provision denying
benefits to an illegitimate born after the start of the parent's disability.

case of the Court's invoking new "fundamental interest" or "suspect classification" ideas to reverse the judgment of *Congress* as expressed in a statute—new Ninth Amendment ideas, as I would call them—we have to look at *Frontiero v. Richardson*[135] and *Weinberger v. Wiesenfeld*, concerning sex discrimination.[136]

It is at least novelistically interesting that the scheme struck down in *Frontiero*, the leading case, was exceeding raw. The woman complaining of discrimination was a navy lieutenant. Under the statute she could contribute just half of her husband's support—an amount not based on her income, but theoretically unlimited, and likely to be quite large if he were sick—and not even get a quarters allowance and medical benefits covering him, while a male lieutenant with a rich wife who actually contributed to his support could get a quarters allowance and medical benefits for her. The question was whether such a rank discrimination was permissible, squarely based as it was on Ms. Frontiero's being female (unless, of course, you are going to hold that having a husband—like pregnancy, in the present Court's view[137]—is not really a sex-linked thing). In the plurality opinion, sex (which, for some peculiar reason, the Court usually, but mercifully not always, calls "gender") is labeled a "suspect" classification.[138] But this conclusion—which would

135. 411 U.S. 677 (1973).

136. 420 U.S. 636 (1975).

137. *Geduldig v. Aiello*, 417 U.S. 484 (1974). The Court sustained the exclusion, from a state disability insurance program, of disabilities accompanying normal pregnancy and childbirth. Said Mr. Justice Stewart: "The lack of identity between the excluded disability and gender [*sic*] as such . . . becomes clear upon the most cursory analysis. The program divides potential recipients into two groups—pregnant women and non-pregnant persons. While the first group is exclusively female, the second includes members of both sexes. The fiscal and actuarial benefits of the program thus accrue to members of both sexes." All this in a footnote. Well, I'll say one thing; that sure was one "cursory analysis"!

138. 411 U.S. at p. 688.

in my frame of thought translate into a conclusion that a broad bar on discrimination against women is a sustainable Ninth Amendment provision—is not attained by flight without instruments into the big sky of prophetic judgment. The Court cites several statutes to establish the acceptance, by Congress, of the principle that sexual employment discriminations are officially frowned on in our society.[139] I could wish that the Court had been more explicit and direct about the quite important issue whether discrimination against blacks may be looked on as a proper first term in analogic reasoning to discrimination against women, with the result that an analogic extension of the real equal protection clause could be projected into the Ninth Amendment. But some of the materials that could support such a judgment—which I, after much thought, believe to be a right one—are alluded to.[140] So is the Nineteenth Amendment,[141] which seems very strongly to imply that in our political society discriminations against women are not only irrational but also unfair.

(I shield myself in parenthesis to wonder if even the most textualist justice would hold, after the Nineteenth Amendment, that women could constitutionally be banned from holding public office. Yet that immunity on their part is not named; if you let in one unnamed right, the game of literalism is up. I wish I could get a town to pass an ordinance saying no woman can be mayor; I'd like to count the Court's votes on that.)

Much might have been made—and might still be made—of the citizenship clause of the Fourteenth Amendment.[142] A good deal might be made, I think, of the fact that this

139. 411 U.S. at p. 687.
140. 411 U.S. at p. 686.
141. 411 U.S. at p. 685.
142. Cf. my STRUCTURE AND RELATIONSHIP IN CONSTITUTIONAL LAW, pp. 51ff (1969); *The Unfinished Business of the Warren Court*, 40 WASHINGTON L. REV. 3, 8ff (1970); Karst, *The Supreme Court 1976 Term. Foreword: Equal Citizenship Under the Fourteenth Amendment*, 91 HARVARD L. REV. 1, especially pp. 53–59 (1977).

discrimination, like other sexual discriminations the Court has
struck down, makes marriage economically difficult for the
female officer and her husband, and penalizes some types of
marital allocation of economic and domestic responsibilities,
and so brings the case within the "autonomy of marriage"
range.

Full argument would be for a thick book rather than for a
lecture, but I think I have mentioned enough possibilities to
suggest that immunity of women from hostile governmental
action may be a requirement of a rational and self-consistent
system—not merely a thing that is wrong because you and I and
Mr. Justice Brennan think it is wrong. But the self-consistency
is the self-consistency of *law*, wherein judgments of the mate-
riality of likenesses and differences have to be made. And these
judgments, here as everywhere in law, are judgments—not
deductions.

The proposed Equal Rights Amendment,[143] which em-
bodies a general judgment of exact relevance, and which would
without question strike down the *Frontiero* discrimination,
seems to me, at the least, to remove from the case altogether any
real conflict with the judgment of Congress. ERA is not valid as
law; this might and I think should make a difference as to some
issues; it is because I do not wish to go into some of those issues
that I have referred to "discrimination against women" rather
than to "discrimination on grounds of sex." But the fact that
two-thirds of each House "deemed it necessary" to propose
ERA[144] is indelibly a fact of record, a fact quite inconsistent
with the supposition that the Court is in *Frontiero* opposing its

143. Section 1 of that proposed amendment reads: "Equality of rights under the
law shall not be denied or abridged by the United States or by any State on account of
sex."

144. "The Congress, whenever two thirds of both Houses shall deem it necessary,
shall propose Amendments to this Constitution. . . ."

own moral judgment to a contrary judgment of the national democratic branch. The decision to banish that fact from view would be a choice, not to defer to Congress, but to exclude as incompetent the best evidence of what Congress thinks, and hence the best evidence of what the country thinks as a political society. One must perceive, as one takes in these facts, that it is not always as obvious as hypothetical and general speculations might make it seem that a judicial judgment striking down an Act of Congress, even on grounds implicating national moral consensus, is a mere howling paradox. There may be all kinds of difficulties here, but they are not difficulties arising either from the absence of material evidence about national consensus, or from a conflict between the Court and Congress on the nature of this consensus. The *Frontiero* problem arose because it came about, in a huge mass of statute law, irregularly reviewed, that a particular provision bluntly contravened a more general ethical judgment officially expressed by Congress in the most serious manner available to that body.

Let me now try to honor the check I gave you on the question of sex as a "suspect classification," so-called, in the process of the review of state laws under the equal protection clause, or of women's "immunity" from sexual discrimination as an "immunity" of national citizenship under the Fourteenth Amendment, or—as I would prefer to say—of such immunity as a Ninth Amendment right. The question whether women's immunity from discrimination is entitled to this status is a national question, a question that asks whether there are lawful grounds, of national scope, for finding this immunity to be one of the "other rights" mentioned in the Ninth Amendment. For the very same reasons that I have just given with respect to the *Frontiero* case itself, we do not have to refer this question to mystical ideas about Western civilization (whose history rarely gives unequivocal support to any very good result, and certainly does not do so in this matter) or about the English-speaking peoples (of whom, in this connection, the less said the better).

I think it legitimate to treat specially the cases of *Bolling v. Sharpe*[145] and *Washington v. Legrant*.[146] *Sharpe* applied the rule of *Brown v. Board of Education*[147] to District of Columbia schools, and *Legrant* held that the District of Columbia Code was subject to the *Shapiro v. Thompson*[148] rule that a year's previous residence might not be required for welfare eligibility. Neither of these cases involved the discernment of special status for the asserted interests on the basis of ethical intuitions or speculations. As to race, little need be said, except that the idea of "suspect classification" is an anachronism in application to *Bolling v. Sharpe*. In those good old days, discrimination against blacks as blacks was *forbidden*. Aside from *Korematsu*, the only leading case that had dealt with race as if it were only a "suspect classification" was *Plessy v. Ferguson*,[149] and even the *Plessy* Court dared not come out and say this plainly—though, allowing for those rougher times, the *Plessy* Court could be said to have found something like a "compelling state interest" in the maintenance of segregation. I'm glad we didn't have the "new" equal protection in 1954.[150]

As to nation-wide mobility, the structural considerations

145. 347 U.S. 497 (1954).

146. 394 U.S. 618 (1969). The reasoning specific to the *Legrant* case is in 394 U.S. at pp. 641–642.

147. 347 U.S. 483 (1954), the leading case holding segregation of black pupils unconstitutional. Since *Brown* was decided under the "equal protection" clause of the Fourteenth Amendment, in its own terms applicable only to the states, the extension of the rule to the District of Columbia was a separate matter.

148. See note 82 above.

149. 163 U.S. 537 (1896). This was the old case upholding segregation—overruled in a line of cases following *Brown v. Board of Education, supra* note 147. On the *Plessy* case see also Introduction, note 2, and *infra* note 159.

150. See above, pp. 45–46.

that give to that right whatever claim it has to being one ought to give it some validity against congressional action.[151]

But another consideration cuts in to both these cases. Where the national power exerts general municipal authority over a territory, very much as a state does, running schools and administering welfare, it ought to be held to the standards binding on the states with respect to matters exactly similar to the ones the states regularly deal with as local authorities. If no such general principle has yet been enunciated, it should be now, on analogic if not on other grounds. If and only if it has rational, equitable warrant, the Ninth Amendment can take it in. The debate on this has revolved around the Court's use, in one of the cases, of the word "unthinkable," to characterize the supposition that Congress should be less limited than the states, merely because the equal protection clause is in its terms applicable only to the states.[152] "Unthinkable" was a disastrous choice of a word, but nothing hinges on that. Right law is not merely the non-unthinkable.

Each of the cases I have mentioned represents an overturning of a formal judgment of Congress. Some people say that Congress has not acted affirmatively to command judicial review of its own actions. But I should think not only that congressional acquiescence in this practice has been so evident that, if the matter were one of private law, one could probably speak of an implied invitation, but also, and more categorically, that the language of Section 25 of the first Judiciary Act,[153]

151. See above at pp. 55–56, and especially the final comment in note 86 above.

152. *Bolling v. Sharpe*, 347 U.S. 497 at 500 (1954).

153. In material part: "Sec. 25. *And be it further enacted*, That a final judgment or decree in any suit, in the highest court of law or equity of a State in which a decision in the suit could be had, where is drawn in question the validity of a treaty or statute of, or an authority exercised under the United States, and the decision is against their validity . . . may be re-examined and reversed or affirmed in the Supreme Court of the United States upon a writ of error. . . ."

unless you approach it with iron determination to make it say something other than what it seems to be saying, did amount (and, as Section 1257 of the Judicial Code,[154] still amounts) to a command to the Supreme Court to affirm such state court judgments, invalidating Acts of Congress, as the Court finds right in law. The question is not whether the material in the Constitution is suitable for use as a basis for thwarting an unwilling Congress, but whether it is suitable as a basis for doing work of which, in a general way, Congress as an official body evidently approves—not as a matter of cloudy inference in pais, not as a matter of fulmination on Capitol Hill for the benefit of constituents, but on the formal record of actions taken, and of actions not taken.

Again we see how closely the question about the powers of Congress over jurisdiction, and the question about the suitability of the constitutional material for use as law in law courts, are intertwined. The effect of congressional acquiescence, amounting very nearly if not entirely to invitation, would approach zero if it became a generally accepted belief that Congress has no choice but to acquiesce. One would have to ask then whether such material as goes into the making of constitutional judgment was suitably definite for interpretation and application by tenured judges, in the teeth of however bitter resentment by the recurrently elected branches, who under the Constitution could do nothing much about it. I have no doubt what my own judgment would be as to "institutional suitability," if the relations of these two institutions were so defined. It is very hard for me to turn my mind, approvingly, toward

154. "§1257. State courts; appeal; certiorari.
Final judgments or decrees rendered by the highest court of a State in which a decision could be had, may be reviewed by the Supreme Court as follows:
    (1) By appeal, where is drawn in question the validity of a treaty or statute of the United States and the decision is against its validity . . .
    (3) By writ of certiorari, where the validity of a treaty or statute of the United States is drawn in question. . . .

constitutional amendment, but that is where I would have to turn it.

The anticipated racing of minutes made me spare you a lengthy introduction—or at least as lengthy a one as I had planned. For a similar reason, I shall spare you a lengthy summing-up—or at least as long a one as I could inflict. To the deeper philosophic and linguistic questions of our century, regarding the name and nature of "decision according to law," I have not been able to say anything. Perhaps nothing general can now be said. I have tried, by illustration, to suggest that the most conspicuous advanced trends of our times, with respect to personal constitutional rights, do not represent a break with law as we know it, in that relative and culture-bound sense in which we do know it. And I have tried, by the implication inherent in my treatment of these illustrations, to give you some of my own views, for what they may be worth to you, concerning the ways in which we may work toward greater lawfulness in these fields, and toward a greater visibility of that lawfulness. I have very clearly implied that—if and only if we can see the judicial authority as constitutionally subject to serious curtailment by the national political branch—the element of reasoning from commitment is, in these materials, enough to go on with.

Some years ago, in the dusk of the entrance to Westminster Hall, a young British politician and I were talking about the Fourteenth Amendment and the British Race Relations Act. With friendly envy, he said to me, "The trouble with us British is that we are not committed to any general principles."[155] How

155. There is now some question whether Britain, by ratifying the European Convention on Human Rights, may have bound herself to observe the broad general principles in that document.

The Irish Constitution of 1937 does commit Ireland to principles of a generality comparable to those of our Constitution, and interpretive problems similar to ours are developing there. See O'Reilly and Redmond, *Cases and Materials on the Irish Constitution* (Law Society of Ireland, Dublin, 1980), *passim;* also Kelly, *The Irish Constitution*, pp. 328 ff (Jurist Pub. Co., Dublin, 1980).

that may be, as to Britain, I say not. As to us, we *are* committed
to general principles, but are always uneasy about it, because if
you are committed to general principles, *which must be vague,*
you never know precisely the full range of your commitment,
and cannot work out the determination of that range by "narrow
verbal criticism."[156] General principles must produce not certainty in law, but uncertainty. Commitment, on the other
hand, means commitment to something. The resolution, such
as it is, can be only along the lines of reasoning from the
commitment, as best one can read it, with all the subtleties and
indeterminacies that have marked legal reasoning from its beginning.

At times, as I have tried to show, the indicated mode of
reasoning generically, but rather closely, resembles common-
law reasoning, in that it asks which result, in the new class of
cases, consists the more easily with the lines and grounds of
decision already committed. Sometimes the indicated mode
may be inference from structure and relation, which one who
enjoyed the intellectual as well as the personal companionship
of Max Gluckman[157] may well believe to be the original source
of law. I conjecture that few if any personal-rights problems will
prove to be entirely out of reach of both these modes. But both
of them do require continual judgments of value, not at large
but within their structures, and material not strictly derived
from either of them must sometimes inform these judgments.
To ask that constitutional law be free of value-judgments thus
implicated is to ask that it not be law. It is crucial, to my
thinking, that the political branches may be seen as continually
permitting and even directing the application of legal methods,

156. The phrase is from Mr. Justice Harlan the elder, in his classic dissent in the
1883 *Civil Rights Cases,* 109 U.S. 3 (1883).
157. See GLUCKMAN, THE IDEAS IN BAROTSE JURISPRUDENCE, *passim* (1965).

such as they are *and can be seen to be*,[158] to the solution of constitutional questions, and they cannot be thought to be doing that if they have no power to constrict the ambit of judicial authority.

Let me emphasize the phrase, "the methods of law, such as they are and can be seen to be." It is my perception, or impression, that much of the more sophisticated literature in this field has drifted toward one of two poles. At one of these, constitutional decision must never be fed by any judgment of rightness, justice, or political wisdom that cannot be rigorously shown to have some kind of objective, quasi-official validation outside the minds and hearts of those who decide. At the other pole, the leeways are seen as plenary, with technicality no longer even a bother; there is hardly a formal difference between saying something is wrong and saying it is unconstitutional.

My belief is that between these poles, not close to either, the art of law is spread out, as the art of music has its life somewhere between traffic noise and a tuning fork—more disciplined by far than the one, with an unfathomably complex inner discipline of its own, far richer than the other, with inexhaustible variety of resource. In the distinctively American decision to submit constitutional questions to law, it is to this art that our political society should be taken to submit them—to this art as it has been, as it is, and above all as it can be seen to be, by those in whose hands lies the decision whether the submission shall continue. It is crucial that our fellow-

158. This point deserves strong emphasis. The First Congress, meeting in 1789, could judge of the propriety of judicial review only on the basis of a 1789 understanding of the legal process. The Ninety-seventh Congress will be able to judge of the propriety of this institution on the basis of 1981 understandings. I do not mean to imply that our insights are necessarily superior, but they are the ones necessarily relevant and operative on the question of "informed consent," by the democracy, to the work of judicial review.

citizens not be misled on this, but possibly the most misleading thing would be to tell them that the submission was to law, when in fact it was to a process at or near either of these poles—because nothing near either of them could be anything like law, as law has been through the ages of humankind.

Vague? Yes. I had far rather be vague than be, as I see it, precise, and precisely wrong. But I do think the vagueness is greatest when one is talking generality, and becomes much less when cases and problems are under scrutiny. That is why I have chosen, in the main, to proceed by example.

One last word: We veterans owe it to younger members of our profession to give them, once in a long while, a look at some of the unprovable judgments experience has brought us to; there is no danger, I am very sure, that they will take these for gospel. As to this present subject, I offer you one of my own—my committed faith, a thing I believe after many years of working and watching. I think that the bow and the string really are related, that attention to the component of even technical reason—which only means close reason—strengthens the justice component. Our earlier shocking dealings with aliens were largely the result of a technical error; we took the sovereign omnipotences of public international law and converted them into omnipotences of Congress, though on the most severely technical level, Congress, as any tolerably well-grounded Austinian will tell you, is not the sovereign, and the sovereign, however hard to locate for all purposes, must be taken to have uttered the Bill of Rights and to have used therein the word "person." *Plessy v. Ferguson*[159] violated the soundest canon of sound law—that decision be taken in knowledge of and with consideration of certainly known facts of public life.[160] The

159. *Supra* notes 2 and 149.
160. See my *The Lawfulness of the Segregation Decisions*, 69 YALE L. J. 421 (1960).

Civil Rights Cases of 1883[161] exhibit shallowness of legal insight and a verbal criticism not only narrow but inattentively and negligently narrow, as in the centrally important failure to deal with the problem of *denial* of equal *protection*. In the long series of "sit-in" cases,[162] I used to hope and pray we would get an adversary who would take strong and skillful issue with the technical points we were making, because I thought we were right, and that the Court would see we were right if the issues could be tautly and clearly drawn.

These are special illustrations. Far more generally, infinitely more deeply, I think the idea itself of justice might never have come into being without the idea of law—that the idea of something's being due is coeval with and eternally bound to the idea that the ascertainment of what is due is a matter of reasoning from commitment—a matter of decision according to law. As with some other precious things, we cannot have this as a sure possession. Let us keep then to its quest.

161. See note 156 above.
162. Those cases wherein black people insisted on service in pubic establishments, and were prosecuted by Southern authorities.